The Road
TO THE Stars

Tom Davies, a Welshman born and bred, trained as a journalist with the *Western Mail* and later worked for *The Sunday Times*, the *Sunday Telegraph* and *The Observer*, where for three years he was the diarist Pendennis. Now a writer, broadcaster and columnist on the *Western Mail*, he has written fourteen books: his *Merlyn the Magician and the Pacific Coast Highway* was short-listed for the Thomas Cook Travel Book of the Year Award, while his pilgrimage narrative *Stained Glass Hours*, published by Triangle in paperback for the first time as *Wild Skies and Celtic Paths*, won the Winifred Mary Stanford prize for the best book with a religious theme. His other best-selling books for Triangle include *Landscapes of Glory* (1996) and *The Celtic Heart* (1997).

Tom recently underwent successful heart surgery and has since started his own political party in Wales, the Celtic Alliance, which hopes to seize control of the new Welsh Assembly and set up a Czech-style artistic republic. He lives in a coastguard tower overlooking the Bristol Channel in Penarth, South Wales and is married with three sons.

The Road
TO THE Stars

TOM DAVIES

TRIANGLE

First published in Great Britain in 1998
Triangle
Society for Promoting Christian Knowledge
Holy Trinity Church
Marylebone Road
London NW1 4DU

British Library Cataloguing-in-Publication Data

A catalogue record for this book is available
from the British Library

ISBN 0-281-05149-6

Typeset by Pioneer Associates, Perthshire
Printed in Great Britain by
Caledonian International, Glasgow

Contents

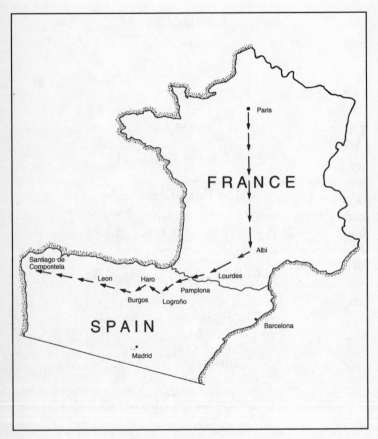

The route of the Pilgrimage

1

A Parisian Dawn

What you notice about the Normandy countryside, almost as soon as you start driving down through her leafy avenues and patchwork of fields, is how you have been there at least a hundred times before. Courtesy of the local fleapit as a child and, later, through far too many hours staring at a television screen, you have been marauding down through these small villages, with ivy shivering on the shuttered walls and advertisements for Dubonnet or Pernod painted on the ends of barns, again and again.

You have fought up and down these roads almost weekly, taken that bridge there – and lost it again – times without number. How often have you been in that wood there for a date with some intrepid members of the Resistance with their great rattling bicycles and radios squealing with static? I must have been in that forest at least a dozen times waiting for some Hooray Henry, with goggles and a white silk scarf, to come parachuting down through the moonlight where-upon I, as the local undercover man, would whisk him off to a distant country rendezvous where he would hide in some farm loft. And, as certainly as night follows day, Henry would fall in love with the farmer's beautiful and sexy daughter and spend the rest of the war learning French so that he would be better able to declare to her, from under several layers of concealing hay, all his troublesome, haunting feelings about war, peace and love which were making him so very sick at heart.

So you just end up standing in these villages in Normandy, outside the *boulangerie* perhaps, with three beefy men in flat caps sitting on a bench and watching you, as you wait for some Nazi tank to come smashing through a wall or some hand grenade to come sailing towards your head or for Errol Flynn or Robert Redford or someone even more unlikely to come running down the road urging on the Dirty Dozen.

And as you stand there, with your imagination locked inside all these daft fantasies, you wish you had never wasted so much time watching those stupid war films. But the fingerprints of war are almost everywhere in this part of the world. On my first night in my Volkswagen camper van in France I woke up in a field next to a giant gun emplacement just outside Boulogne. This turned out to be the *Musée du Mur de L'Atlantique* which contained a vast collection of land-mines, gas rattles and guns – everything designed in an obviously old-fashioned way, completely removed from our modern high tech world, to generate as much death and violence as possible. There were also wax dummies of the Nazi gunners lying in their bunks inside the emplace-ment or sitting around tables and I was to learn from the women in the ticket kiosk that the whole operation was owned by a Welshman who also gloried in the surname of Davies.

Although I was not to know it at the time this was to be the beginning of a month of storms over France. One moment you could be marvelling at the huge balls of sun-shine rolling slowly around you and the swallows flying high as the heat baked the silky green corn spattered with the red puffs of many poppies. But then mists would begin to thicken in a distant dip in the hills with dark pillars taking shape in these mists as the air grew chillier with the swallows flying closer to the ground – or retiring from their zanily fluttering flights altogether – as the cows moved towards the shelter of stone walls.

Those pillars of mist became darker still and the first drops of cold rain pattered lightly on your outstretched palm. A wind moaned with real feeling when – *swoosh!* – everything began going mad at about the same time with forks of lightning stammering silently and huge rumbles of thunder, with truly apocalyptic muscles on them, shaking the earth repeatedly. All these furious elements kept edging ever closer towards little old you, standing there with bated breath and wondering if, at any second now, you were going to be turned into a small bit of charcoaled toast.

We can see some of the many faces of God in these days of sudden storms, ranging from his majestic serenity to the terrible quickness of his wrath. Just before the storm there was his utter calm and the steadfastness of his spacious love. His holy perfection was stretched right across those sunny fields of young corn.

But then his more hidden and elusive qualities began coming together in the air. Lightning and thunder destroyed the calm. Warmth turned to cold and, as if from nowhere, we were confronted with a huge and dark explosion of wrath which even filled the swallows with alarm.

Martin Luther characterized God's love as his 'proper' work and his wrath as his 'strange' work. We can see, then, in the sunshine and thunder of a day of the storm, something of the very heart of God; we can sense something of the awesome conflict deep within his very being.

In God's 'proper' work we can usually locate the image and activity of his son Christ, the shelter from the storm. But in his 'strange' work there is his ungovernable fury, the place of tempest where darkness is locked in a ferocious battle with light. In Christ we have shelter; outside Christ we risk injury from the full blast of God's wrath.

We need to keep a wary eye on the strangeness and unpredictability of God, I believe. We need to learn to live in fear of him again, remembering his absolute holiness and invincible purity, because it is these very qualities which can make him dangerous. He may be sunnily calm on this Normandy morning but, when his sense of his own holiness is unendurably violated, he can turn to savage tempest. His purity is of paramount importance to him but, if his world begins threatening his sense of his own purity, we can only expect trouble on the largest scale. Judgements of flame and flood will rain down from which there will be no shelter.

But not today in Northern France, not yet since the storm soon abated and shafts of sunlight broke through the clouds, lighting up the cornfields in a honey fire and telling us of God's transcendent goodness and infinite patience with his broken and fallen world.

It had just gone three o'clock in the morning, with rain falling steadily on the crooked rooftops and gurgling cobbles as I drove slowly up through Montmartre in Paris, stopping here and there to watch the events of the street on this wet, summer night in the City of Love.

A tangle of accordion music disappeared in the rain and a distant *chanteuse* was singing sweetly about *l'amour* as I passed the cemetery and carried on up the hill to the Basilica of Sacré Cœur as she sat gazing out over the sleeping city, mistily luminous beneath all her orange night lights. In a way I was actually sneaking into one of my favourite cities, almost like a thief setting out to burgle her soul under the cover of darkness since I had long known, from bitter and deafening experience, how Paris can resemble the shrieking corridors of Bedlam during the day but also how she can become a beautiful and gracious queen who is actually prepared to give you a personal audience if you are quiet and gentlemanly about it and come before her throne, cap in hand and on your own, in a spirit of homage and late at night.

Yet even at this hour there were pockets of activity in the odd dancing room even if most of the restaurants were shuttered and quiet with the dripping chairs piled up high outside them and all locked together. The rain kept washing over the cobbles and splattering down the drains. A patrolling gendarme watched my hesitant progress carefully as a woman walked past him exercising her poodle and enjoying this abandoned night.

The rain emptied down the walls of the Sacré Cœur, rushing out of gargoyled mouths and splattering over the outlying cemetery. A few floors up one building, above a shop, a man, a black shadow in a white vest, was looking out over the city from his balcony with his hands close together. A couple of *clochards* moved around in the damp darkness of a doorway; rumpled and helpless shadows who, I hoped, had taken enough *vin* to keep them warm and happy this cold, wet night in the city. That accordion again.

I pulled up at a junction to sit and watch the comings and goings in the street. Odd cars zipped past with their speeding tyres smashing up the puddles and there was an irregular procession of drunks too, heading home sideways or backwards, one falling into dustbins or bashing his head against lamp-posts but still, somehow, keeping going. Even in his parlous state he seemed to understand that you just can't lie down and sleep it off in all this rain or else it would be a case of hypothermia mingled with pneumonia and a touch of frost-bite all adding up to an early booking in the local cemetery.

I drove down to the lovely gardens of the Tuileries, where flowers stood around their beds in military precision and a sodden couple, clearly entering into the spirit of the place, were kissing in the rain on a park bench. A shrieking girl, her white dress soaked through, went running past the kissing couple and, about five seconds later, a man rose up out of the dripping darkness, chasing after her.

The thing about all this rain was that it seemed to neutralize all the other sounds, occasionally letting a snatch of music through or the rumble of a distant dust cart or a shout of glee but, mostly, allowing only the sound of the city. Paris had never seemed quite so peaceful or magical with the street lights dancing on the moving water in the gutters.

The minute detail of the ironwork also shone out through the damp darkness on every corner – the winged *pissoirs*, the arrowhead railings and the huge variety of plain and ornamental door knobs, each of them as individual as a human fingerprint. Along with this extravagant ironwork was the crookedness of everything; the inability of doors to stand up straight or for walls to be tidily vertical or the window sills to do anything other than sag forlornly like the very oldest old age pensioner. These houses were built to look a hundred years old. They were first put up to appear as though they were about to fall down again. They dripped with their own charm and the unmistakable smell of lots of money.

The mighty shape of the Cathedral of Notre Dame – where Napoleon was once crowned Emperor of France – can lift up your eyes and soul like no other. You can stand next to the Seine, swollen and relentless with so much rain, and make out her lofty shape in the drizzle. Gargantua and the hunchback trooped around those spiky towers and above that moon-like window. Rain kept smashing down through the light of the street lamps as I raised my fist to salute this mother of churches. 'A vast symphony in stone,'

wrote Victor Hugo. 'A human creation as powerful and
fecund as the divine creation.'

But, for our immediate purposes, there is a much more
interesting church nearby, in the centre of medieval Paris,
in the shape of Saint-Jacques-de-la-Boucherie in the Rue
Saint-Jacques where a lone man, even now and at this
unearthly hour, was walking down the pavement, in the
darkness, carrying a rolled-up carpet on his shoulder. This
is one of the oldest of the city churches with an elegant
Gothic belfry and a statue of St Jacques – or St James as he
is known to *les anglais* – on one of her spires. The church
is one of the main starting places for French pilgrims going
to Compostela where they would have gathered largely
from Flanders, Artois or Picardy before setting out on their
perilous journey to Galicia in North West Spain. And it
was here that my own pilgrimage began in earnest.

By the year 1000 there were three main pilgrimages in
Christendom: to Jerusalem, Rome and Santiago de Compostela. The years 1000 to 1500 were the heyday of pilgrimage
with many pilgrims braving extreme dangers to reach the
grail of their religious dreams. The pilgrimage to
Compostela offered a difficult and adventurous journey
particularly as Spain was locked in a long war with the
Moors who, after taking Jerusalem, were anxious to extend
their sacred Islamic kingdom. But danger was particularly
attractive to the early pilgrims who had no fear of dying *en
route* because they knew their departing souls would have
been covered in glory.

The body of St James, one of Jesus' disciples, had been
mysteriously brought to Spain from the Holy Land and
taken to Santiago. It duly disappeared, only to be 'found'
again by a monk following a wandering star in Galicia.
This 'find' was rapturously welcomed by the king of Spain
and St James heroically came to the aid of Christian Spain
in her struggle with the Islamic Moors. The saint even

appeared in the thick of battles with the Moors, taking the historical role of Moorslayer who saved the country in the *Reconquista*. In one battle in the Ebro Valley the saint appeared on a white charger brandishing a sword with which he beheaded numerous Moors.

The news of his reappearance spread through Europe and pilgrims began trickling down to Spain. Charlemagne and his paladins were among the first attracted by his cult when they also began doing battle with the Moors. A shrine built to St James in Compostela by a thankful Spanish Royal family has been sacked many times down the ages. By the start of the ninth century the pilgrimage to Compostela had begun in earnest and still continues to this day despite war, famine and the Reformation which insisted that it should come to an end. The Wife of Bath in Chaucer's *Canterbury Tales* had, she said, been 'thrice to Jerusalem, at Rome, at Boloyne and in Galice at Seynt Jame'.

Archbishop Gelmirez in Galicia used the pilgrimage to promote his bishopric around 1100 when the shrine became a rallying symbol against the Moors. Pilgrim hospices and churches were built along The Road. The Royal families of Leon and Castile poured in riches taken in tribute from the Moors. French monks and priests became welcome guests. The cathedrals of Leon and Burgos were built and many of the churches along The Road were endowed with their own 'authentic' reliquary. Jerusalem had been lost to Islam and so the pilgrimage to Compostela prospered with hundreds of thousands setting out on it every year looking for yet more glory for their souls.

One of the world's first guide books was about this pilgrimage, the *Liber Sancti Jacobi*, written by Ameri Picaud, a monk, in 1140, part of a five-volume work, the *Codex Calixtus*, which details the full story of the life and legends of St James.

There are now an astonishing million or so people a year making this journey which traditionally began in a number of French cities including Vezelay, Le Puy, Arles and here in Paris. These roads meander across the face of France like so many varicose veins before coming together near the Pyrenees where they take more or less the same road across the north of Spain to Compostela, the traditional resting place of St James, the Son of Thunder, the Apostle with the Fiery Heart.

On a pilgrimage like this, one may set out to search for the tempestuous character of St James but such a journey might also be a switchback ride into anything from praise to fear, adventure or faith. We will be sniffing at real and bloody history too, passing through Roncesvalles where Roland, in charge of Charlemagne's rearguard, fell; through Viana where Cesare Borgia lies and thence to Burgos, home of Rodrigo Diez de Vivar, better known as El Cid or even better known as Charlton Heston.

Along with the cities and countryside we will be exploring ourselves too, teasing out connections between holy places and our own spiritual journey, looking directly at our personal relationship with God and weighing it against that of others. We will also be learning something about our own fears and seeking to confront and overcome them.

So a pilgrimage is as much a journey of the mind and an exploration of ourselves as it is an adventure across a landscape or a passage through history. It's a re-run of scenes from our lives, thoughts of our past loves and hates and chats with God about how, perhaps, he might have ordered things a better way. It's a way, too, of building a picture of him in our minds so that we might come closer to the beat of his heart.

There are more layers to a modern pilgrimage than the largest Spanish onion and it is emphatically not some harrowing mortification of the body which was once so central to the medieval concept of pilgrimage. We are not out here barefoot on our knees or crawling mile after mile with our minds focused solely on the suffering of the Cross as we wait for some marauding Moor to do us in.

On this journey, which can be fun as well as devotional, comfortable as well as painful, we should open ourselves out to almost everyone and anything The Road may present. It's the people we meet and the scrapes we get into; the meditations on a landscape we might have and the visions we might see; all the odd, small things we learn – about the world and ourselves.

You might, for example, have wondered what happened to Bo Diddley. I had long thought he was doing a gig in the great rock 'n' roll concert in the sky but he was actually to be seen rocking in Le Puy later that month, according to a poster I spotted on the road out of Paris. Also if you ever wondered what happened to Patrick Duffy of *Dallas* fame, as I do about every 22 years, I can tell you here and now that he is alive and well and soon to be singing in a Country and Western Music Festival in Auch, according to another poster on the same road.

I wonder if Patrick ever sings my all-time Country and Western favourite: 'Take Your Tongue Out Of My Mouth Because I'm Kissing You Goodbye'.

The first stop on the pilgrim road to Compostela reared up from the flat countryside south of Paris like an unexpected element in a strange dream. It had a green roof with buttressed walls and two spires – one plain and the other ornamental – scraping the low blue sky.

I am here forever and you, pilgrim stranger, can pass through and glory in my intricate wonders, the cathedral of Chartres said. Come close to me, the very palace of the Queen of Heaven, and perhaps you will even learn something about God himself. The closer you got, the clearer the details from the opulent shapes of the windows and the abundance of the tiny sculptured figures on the walls which tell the many stories under heaven about the complicated life here on this earth.

But the essence of Chartres, I believe, is light. It was built in celebration of Jesus Christ – 'the light of the world' – who so briefly and gloriously illuminated the darkness at the centre of time. You notice this light largely because of its absence as you step into the cathedral's dark and shadowy interior. This echoey murk makes you squint as you try and work out what's what until you lift your eyes and behold the multi-coloured magnificence of the stained glass windows. Clouds move across the face of the sun outside and, inside, the light moves with it. Shafts of light roll across the transept and hit the stone columns. The statues on the baroque altar seem to be defying gravity as they hang in the light pouring down from the clerestory windows.

Here is an extraordinary creation which tells you something about the medieval perception of God as a vast darkness with shafts of light moving around inside it in which, sometimes, you might be able to lie like a cat basking in a pool of sunshine. But, more often than not, it was a place where you were left alone and chattering in cold winds.

Even the story of Christ's first coming was told in the sweeps of light and colour in the Rose Window which faces west where the sun sets in the evening of time. The Old Testament figures on the dark side of the cathedral run into New Testament figures on her bright side. But one window emphasizes the medieval view of the unity of the testaments and how they are different sides of the same coin.

These windows, which the sunlight kept changing and moving around, were peopled by big-eyed prophets, stories from the Bible and complicated family trees. Here also angels fluttered in frozen flight, whales vomited up small hapless figures and a motley parade of money changers, fishmongers and vintners went about their business in a complicated narrative which mirrored the sweep of a restless and industrious humanity.

Exactly as you were doing, so had millions of pilgrims down the years before you looked up, seeing their favourite stories brought to life in such brilliant and vivacious colours that they might live in their minds forever. So you were walking around in a sort of medieval CD-ROM, a giant living encyclopaedia, set out in the most careful and painstaking detail like the 41 sculptured tableaux on that choir screen, so intricate it took 200 years to complete.

This sacred place managed to survive centuries of modernization, revolution and war, the guide told us. The stained glass windows were numbered and moved to safety in the last war and it took four years to put them back. They also had a hospital here for the stained glass, successfully treating a fungus on the windows which had been discovered. That beautiful velvet red was obtained by putting thin layers of red nitrate on either side of the glass. The chalk stone of the choir screen had to be cleaned continuously because of the dust from visitors' shoes.

The star relic here was the Sancta Camisia, thought to be the garment worn by Mary when she gave birth to Christ. It was presented to the cathedral by Charles the Bald in 876 and thus this place has come to be known as the earthly palace of the Queen of Heaven, a fabled palace of darkness and light where you can stand around and sense something of the mystery and strangeness of God himself.

2

A Cure in Lourdes

Towards the end of the afternoon, just before dinner, we wandering campers like to pull into a camp site or a farm in our vans, where we usually scatter to the far corners of some dung-littered field, prepare our dinner and watch the sun go down with a little *vin*.

Last night, on a farm in the Dordogne, just as the sun was dipping out of the day, one of the van doors opposite me opened and a fat woman with an even fatter smile emerged, holding out a cake with three lighted candles on it. She crossed the field, closely followed by her husband who was playing an accordion, both of them looking like swaggering, flamboyant silhouettes from a Walt Disney cartoon. On the other side of the field they were received by a group with much clapping and whooping and they sat around a table and caroused until late.

My sleep was unusually restless that night since I had left one of my van windows slightly open and was visited by a mosquito in the darkness, first hearing him whining in my ear like some errant kamikaze plane which had lost its way to the war. Panic stations as the light went on and I was on full alert with a can of Raid in my hand. However, he had scarpered and so, after a few hopeful squirts into a few likely corners, I settled back into my sleeping bag and turned

13

off the light but, within a minute or so, he was back screaming and poised to attack.

After failing to get him once more I turned my light off
again and wriggled deep down into my sleeping bag,
pulling the hood up over my head and tying it up so tight
that only my nose was poking up out of the air, when the
little sod flew down through the darkness with an accuracy
that suggested he knew enough about radar to interest the
Royal Air Force, landed right on the tip of my nose and
gave it a really good bite, only to take off again before I
could free my arms sufficiently to get him.

When the sun climbed over the Dordogne, as it did
between the storms, it roasted the countryside with a trop-
ical ferocity. You could almost see the growth in the cornfields, the flowered gardens and the tumbling butterflies.
The eaves of the houses were abrim with swallows tending
their noisy nests and, out in the woods, buzzards hunted,
woodpeckers drilled and a wild deer broke sudden cover to
stand blinking in a clearing like a hunted fugitive before
diving deep back into the undergrowth again. This is *foie
gras* country and every so often you could see those luckless geese striding pugnaciously across a meadow clearly
unaware of what the local peasants were planning to do
with their exploded liver.

When you do a lot of standing around on your own and
just looking – as I can do for hour after hour – you also get
a lot of people giving you a right good looking back, like
the woman standing in her garden with a weeding fork in
her hand or the young, black-eyed French girl framed in her
own doorway and of such striking beauty you feel her gaze
might well follow you for mile after mile, hour after hour
or even year after year.

The next night I stood in a wood for a while listening to
the sounds – the winds shivering the leaves, the bark of a
fox, the rumble of distant storms and the odd cries of pain

searing the purple and black shadows. Everything on legs was up and about in those shadows, as could be seen the next morning from the myriad wild animals who ended up drowned in one of the local swimming pools.

Such moments of night music can be moments of worship too as you let your senses run free and you try and become as one with the natural world and everything that is growing and moving so busily all around you. When you make that connection it is also possible to connect with God as he pumps furious smelts of creative energy into every nook and corner of his great creation. As you look around, you will see his universal godhood in the eyes of the foxes and feel it in the brush of cobwebs on your cheeks and hear it in the cries of pain in those purple shadows and in the sounds of distant storms threatening another of their tumultuous and operatic performances.

After travelling through France extremely slowly for three weeks and getting lost regularly since I cannot read maps, I realized I had got as far as Périgueux and had still not yet met a single pilgrim, with the traditional walking staff in his hand and scallop shell dangling around his neck, making his way to Compostela.

But I had met a few really strange characters like the Welsh builder who was developing some farm buildings down this way and whose idea of speaking French was to speak English very loudly with a French accent. He had imported some other Welsh labourers and his farm had become a sort of Welsh *Auf Wiedersehen Pet* with them all getting drunk first thing in the morning and nothing getting built. Everything on the farm looked either broken or about to fall down and there was usually a comatose figure or three lying out in his field at almost any time of day. 'They are used to watery beer back home,' the gaffer explained, 'and this French wine is really killing them.'

Drink was taking its toll in other ways. In a Limoges bar

there was a man with vertically sloping shoulders and a huge mournful face who pestered everyone. He was the local drunk, *le patron* explained, who had once got on his scooter, fallen off and ended up upside down in a drainage ditch. The gendarmes breathalysed him after he was lifted out of the ditch by his ankles and he was summoned to court but was too drunk to turn up. He was duly sentenced to two months imprisonment, a sentence he quite enjoyed.

One of my favourite characters was Steve, a young Londoner whom I met while waiting to weigh some fruit in a supermarket in Brive. We had a cup of coffee together and, as we chatted, I noticed that every so often he punched his left side with his fist. *Pourquoi?*

Well, he said, he'd had a serious injury to his side and the doctors had installed some sort of pacemaker to keep his injured bits ticking over. He didn't think the thing worked properly so he kept punching it to keep it going. He had been driving his lorry to Lyons, he added, and there'd been a bit of a bump whereupon his front wheel had gone rolling down the road in front of him. Now whereas you and I might just sit there and look on such a happening with quiet amazement Steve immediately braked and leaped out of his cab to give chase to the runaway wheel. He failed to stop it with his hands so, extremely stupidly he now accepted, he stood side on in front of it and ended up getting run over by his own runaway wheel.

Saint Cécile Cathedral in Albi, another traditional stop on the road to Compostela with its own pilgrim chapel for St James, is not so much a church as a monstrous brick battle-ship which steams across the sky high up above the roofs of the city, as befits a building which was once conceived as a massive weapon of war to defend the city and preserve her faith. You can still find defence battlements in her huge opulent doorway with its richly decorated canopy and there was once a prison in the adjoining tower.

But, inside, her atmosphere changes and you encounter strange and delicately patterned walls and chapels, you see a high vaulted ceiling flooded with azure blue and gold, you wander the Great Choir and study the many and varied chiselled figures on the rood screen. The Psalm Book of gold and lace tells of the magnificent glory of God. The huge detailed painting of The Last Judgement, thought to be one of the largest single pictures in the world, is a dazzling portrait of mankind on the run, a vast and compelling argument for God and the assembly of his people.

It is a place which, like many of her sister cathedrals, repays hours of careful inspection and prayerful meditation. There is something interesting in every corner but what I thought was that here, again, we find a building which is also a vast metaphor for the complex personality of God and the way he is both a destroyer and creator, the one side of his character often battling with the other. History, in a sense, has been the long and bloody saga of a God working out his own inner contradictions in relationship to his people with whom he constantly identifies and suffers and here was another pointer to that mysterious tale.

In the huge and war-like exterior of the cathedral we meet the furious and powerful God of the Old Testament, the one who flooded the world, levelled Sodom, destroyed the enemies of Israel and then, touchingly, regretted it. This was a God who was a warrior at heart, conquering Egypt and destroying the Canaanites. This was a God who could be awesomely truculent, once turning a woman into a block of salt. He would go quiet for long periods and then explode into an awesome rage. When Moses asked him who he was he said, with the tremendous self-confidence we can see in the exterior of this cathedral: 'I am what I am.'

But as we wander through the interior and revel in her artistic creations, based on the somewhat gentler testimony of the New Testament, we see something of a more solicitous God and the way he can become a friend to the friendless. This is a God who can also be exceptionally tender, a personal advocate and law-giver, a comforter in times of grief.

So Saint Cécile Cathedral in Albi tells us something about the size, the colour and the shape and the personality of our Father, not as some bearded old duffer sitting on a throne in the clouds with dutiful cherubim tending the corns on his feet, but as a large and complex Father destined to be our Father forever, red in tooth and claw, patron of fine art and destroyer of his enemies, a devoted shepherd and an indulgent uncle, who is working out his destiny in relationship to his stumbling, failing people who keep breaking the covenant which he once imposed on them in the life and death of his only son.

There is a serene and deeply spiritual quality about many of the faces painted by Henri de Toulouse-Lautrec and now on display in the Berbie Palace in Albi just over the road from the cathedral. Their humanity remained tangled in my mind for ages – the cold, knowing eyes of the prostitute, the weakness and even despair of the doctor, the vivacity and movement of the dancers in the *Folies Bergère*, the intimacy of the woman making up her face in a mirror, the blowsy freshness of the English actress in Le Havre. 'The face alone exists,' said Toulouse-Lautrec.

Here was a painter who depicted the whole gamut of the human comedy with a scalpel precision and what I particularly admired in his art was that it was devoid of priggishness. He could portray dancers, lesbians and prostitutes without a trace of moral loftiness, embracing their every spirit with an unflinching humanity while also immortalizing their human ordinariness.

Christ also moved among ruffians, deviants and prostitutes without needing to stand in judgement over them. A prig was the last thing he was, a point which seems to have got lost on many of his po-faced and stiff-necked followers.

French drivers are among the most impatient anywhere, make no mistake. I could be trundling down through a lovely avenue of rustling elms and past enticing restaurants, having a bit of a daydream, with Bruce Springsteen singing a nice love song to me on my cassette player, as he often does when I am driving, when I will become aware of a small car buzzing from side to side behind me (it is almost always a small car with a smoking exhaust and several bits hanging off, driven by some would-be Grand Prix maniac hunched over the wheel), one second on my nearside window and the next in the off, tooting for an opening and clearly about to explode with an incendiary rage since I just might be about to shave all of 30 seconds off the precious gift that is his life.

He toots and I ignore him since my van is a good deal bigger than his little car and Bruce keeps singing to me. He toots again and I maintain my line on the road as Bruce plays me one of his truly wonderful guitar solos. More enraged toots follow so I finally move over to let him go past, giving him a little satirical toot of my own and, as he accelerates off, in another puff of black smoke, busily winding down his window, it's no end of waving fists, filthy gestures and obscene signs which would have got him shot at dawn in Singapore.

But, apart from a few of their nuttier drivers, I am quite fond of the French despite their general tendency towards smugness and superiority. They seem a race at ease with themselves and you can usually be sure of a cheery 'Bonjour' or a 'Bon appétit' as I once got simply because I was standing in a garage forecourt sucking an ice lolly. They are not especially criminal or violent and, whenever they meet, it's handshakes and lots of kisses all round. They are forever playing with their children in such a smiling, cheerful manner it suggests they are really enjoying rather than enduring it.

They also seem to have a real religious sensibility, fond of their churches and the practice of prayer. Almost every other field has a wooden cross on its borders or some kind of shrine on the road put there, perhaps, in memory of a crash victim. Their cemeteries are pretty sumptuous productions too: big tombs, many regularly festooned with fresh flowers. These are a people who are not about to forget their dead.

The only really black mark I would put against them is their fondness for little dogs, with their mad haircuts and diamanté collars, nothing more than useless, coiffed yapping machines on leads who seem to keep yapping, morning, noon and night, even when they are supposed to be asleep.

Beyond Toulouse I picked up the road to the Pyrenees, which marked the Spanish border. Those storms were still building up and sweeping down over the lush green parallelograms of the vineyards with the quick winds making the tops of the vines dance around like so many slam-dancing youngsters out on an all-night rave.

Sun. Rain. Sun. It had become almost impossible to predict how this weather would go; one minute it was pouring with rain and the next the boiling hands of the sun would grab the throat of the land again, shaking out many competing fragrances and fluttering insects with no end of bees and gnats. I watched any hornet that went hammering past with particular care since a sting from that could kill a young horse.

When the rain returned it washed all those fragrances back into the earth before setting up a warm, damp canopy of nothingness over the steaming land which tasted faintly of ice cream. Even the many insects cleared off to find shelter in the rain, often finding their way into the houses since insects don't like getting wet any more than we do.

Interspersed throughout the vineyards were fields of giant marigolds with their dark moon faces looking up at the sun like an assembly of schoolboys slightly in awe at the magnificence of their headmaster. But, when the rain started again, these attentive schoolboys became an assembly of disgraced ones as they stood with their heads bowed and petals in disarray. The faces of those marigolds didn't follow the sun all the time either, I noticed, since they sometimes turned away at the end of the afternoon, almost as if they'd had enough ultra-violet for one day.

But there are strange elements in this landscape too, like a tower on stilts in the middle of a field of lavender or a small wood and brick square box on stone pillars on the summit of that hill. These tiny buildings became even more arresting at night when sheet lightning picked them out standing alone in the fields like – well what? – well, like small churches that never quite grew into big churches or baby castles that never quite managed to become adult castles or even watchtowers long since abandoned by their watchmen. They made no sense, these tiny neo-chapels, some rackety and the others restored, trooping across vinous horizons and useless for almost anything and anyone, particularly a moment of quiet prayer. One night I spotted one with a fire beneath it and it looked like some ominous primordial symbol; a prehistoric flying saucer which had crash-landed and was going up in flames.

These, I soon discovered, were the pigeon-houses of the Midi – once packed with a burbling, fluttering population reared for fertilizer, food and flying messages over enemy lines – and now but empty shells, often decorated with pinnacles, crosses or ornamental animals and many with mushroom stone caps on the tops of their pillars to stop rats climbing up and stealing the pigeon eggs. They no longer have any use and stand dotted around the country-side looking mysterious; stone anachronisms, architectural hiccups, left alone like dwellings hoping forlornly for the return of some dwellers mad enough to want to dwell in them again.

The misty sky above the Pyrenees was vibrant with rainbows as I drove into Lourdes, noticing this was a place set apart with its massing profusion of advertisement hoardings, hotels and pointless shops, the likes of which I had not seen in rural France but had noticed a lot in California.

The thronging streets spoke of commercial crookedness and headaches without end and I kept looking up longingly at the wildness and freedom of the outlying mountains which seemed like huge and dark hump-backed whales, frozen there for all time as they dived again into that sea of rainbows and mists. Down here it was a traffic jam looking for the release of half a dozen car parks with the shops packed to their roofs with piles of glittering rubbish. A man was hanging on to a huge bunch of red, helium balloons shaped like human hearts and, just near him, another was making a call on a mobile phone.

A closer look at the shops revealed their true horror: the T-shirts, the gilt crucifixes, the plastic holy water bottles, the pious bracelets, the bum-bags, the stamps, the postcards, the medallions, the pots, the pens, the Lourdes dolls, the perfumes, the coloured pebbles, the Holy Mother with a halo of winking lights (batteries not included).

Some four million pilgrims a year come here to Lourdes, making it the largest pilgrim centre in the world, even including Mecca. And here they all were milling around me now: a screeching mob of boys and girls in national costume from Zagreb; Breton pastors jangling their rosaries; wrinkled peasant French women dressed completely in black; shouting Scots from Glasgow; ruddy-faced priests from Ireland probably with a weakness for hard drink; young women from Spain with armfuls of babies; fat Italian mamas with flabby pasta muscles and dancing Spaniards from Barcelona plainly around the bend ... wave after wave of them, the whole shuffling army of God, come by rail, road or air to pay their respects to a famous place of healing where, in the famine year of 1858 a frail young girl, Bernadette Soubirous, saw a heavenly vision which not only shook her but went on to shake the world.

She was out gathering firewood, the story goes, when she saw an apparition of the Virgin Mary in the mist, high above a rock in a grotto. The Lady spoke to the child saying: 'Please come here every day for a fortnight. Tell the priests to build a chapel on this spot. Prayer and penitence! Go and drink in the spring and wash in it. I am the Immaculate Conception.'

The Lady pointed out a spring which became a stream and soon crowds began gathering regularly around a rude shelter. Miracles took place. A blind man washed his eyes in the water and saw again. The son of Napoleon III was cured and a new centre for pilgrimage grew up here.

A four-year commission of investigation by the Catholic Church came up with a complete vindication of Bernadette's story and, in 1862, the Bishop of Tarbes and Lourdes issued a decree saying that the apparition was real and the faithful were justified in believing it certain. Bernadette died in Nevers in 1879 and was canonized in 1933. Soon this strange place of candles and prayer was to become unofficially incorporated into the pilgrimage to Compostela.

I parked and threaded my way down through the crowds

towards the Basilica where thousands of people were milling around the outskirts of the empty forecourt and the amplified tenor voice of a priest was lifting up through the trees. This area around the Basilica, the Domaine, was like some huge spiritual funfair with different activities going on in almost every part of its 30 acres. Everywhere you looked there was something beautiful – from the fat trout rising to take the insects in the clear river to wagon after wagon of guttering candles around Bernadette's grotto. Somehow – and I am not at all sure how – the Church authorities had managed to maintain the integrity of the Domaine since there were no conventional shops anywhere and not a single advertisement in sight. Green lawns spread out between high trees with statues of the Archangel Raphael, protector of travellers, Gabriel opening his book and Michael crushing Satan under his foot.

The Procession of the Blessed Sacrament was about to start and the first of a great crocodile of wheelchairs began rolling into the forecourt in front of the Basilica, accompanied by a peal of bells. That tenor voice rose up again and a white drift of nurses swept through the crowd. A baby near me was grizzling unhappily.

I wanted to get nearer to the altar to watch the service but was stopped by one of the volunteer *brancardiers* holding a rope. 'Mais je suis un journaliste,' I said hopefully, a ploy that sometimes opens doors because everyone is afraid of upsetting the Press. Everyone, that is, except this man.

'Non, non. Pour les malades.'

'Je suis malade.'

'Vous êtes journaliste.'

'Oui, oui. Je suis un journaliste et je suis malade and je needs to get closer to the altar to see what's going on.'

'Non, non. N'est pas possible. Allez-vous en.'

He actually pointed to where I should stand and I duly stood there feeling foolish as I again tried to work out what was happening. By now, I guessed, there were some 3,000 sufferers in wheelchairs lined up in front of the Basilica and they had been struck down and torn apart by some of the deadliest diseases known to man. Faces were deformed and tongues lolling. Backs were hunched and legs but twisted stumps. Some were blind and others wore deaf-aids. Vacant faces stared blankly and wildly. But this was Lourdes. This was the last port of them all and these invalids had come with a gambler's hope in their hearts; all in the market for a miracle. *Lord, they whom thou lovest are sick.*

A further chorus of prayers and pleas fluttered in the air as the choir began singing. Over on a distant hill was a fort which was taken by the Moors back in 800. Charlemagne then laid siege to it and the Saracen chief capitulated before becoming a Christian and Lourdes' first governor. *Lord, the blind whom thou lovest want to see.*

The Sacred Host was held up over every sick person. Another huge prayer rolled up to the very gates of heaven. Rosaries were held out and hands held high. Next a great silence trawled through the world as their eyes widened with a hope – a terrifying hope they might be made whole again.

But no miracles were on offer in the market today even if the spirits of the invalids seemed visibly lifted as they were wheeled away to the accompaniment of a sweetly sorrowing gypsy violin. In its 100 years of business more than 5,000 cures have been recorded by the Lourdes Medical Bureau, with 64 having been pronounced miracles. Most of these cures have taken place during this service and, just behind the officiating priest, a small group of doctors had waited and observed. *Lord, that I may hear.*

Yet as I was left alone in the rapidly thinning crowds I was feeling as confused as at any time in my confused life. The problem was I really hadn't lied to that *brancardier*

since I was seriously *malade* myself and if you were wondering why I wasn't doing this pilgrimage to Compostela as
I was supposed to – on my own two feet or, at the very
least, on a bicycle – it was because I had a heart condition
and a serious operation beckoned. One of my coronary
veins was shot, with two others on the blink. This being
Thatcher's Britain, where you can get almost anything if
you can pay for it, the waiting list was waiting forever
and, meanwhile, I was finding it difficult to get up any sort
of hill and any reasonable sort of walk reduced my legs
to lead. Few pilgrims in the long and arduous history of
pilgrimage could have been quite as knackered as me and I
could no more have walked to Compostela than climbed
Everest which was why I was doing this one in a camper
van in which I could always pull over and snatch a little
snooze whenever I got too tired.

The reason for my confusion here in Lourdes, then, was
that I was not at all sure how I should behave in a place of
healing. What, if anything, should I ask for? Should I go
down on my knees right now and ask God to sort out my
arteries? And how might I put it? Now it may have been
something to do with my own lack of faith or it may have
been something to do with unanswered prayers in the past
or it may have been something to do with a more or less
perpetual sense of guilt about not being a good enough
Christian – whatever a good enough Christian might be –
or else it might have been all these factors rolled into
one – plus a few I had not yet thought of – but here in
Lourdes, in a famous place of healing, I did not know why
or how I should petition God, if indeed I should petition
him, since I have always had an instinctive belief in God's
better judgement. I was sure he knew when I was going to
fall off my perch and there was absolutely nothing all the
prayers in the world could – or should – do about it.

So it was with a strange and undecisive unease that I

stood there looking in the direction of the Pyrenees, with that *brancardier* still eyeing me suspiciously, as if I was about to start some trouble, wondering what to do next when, right at that moment, my unformed prayers were answered and I received what I still consider to be a miracle cure, even if the Lourdes Medical Bureau might have a few problems with it.

I turned and spotted a small figure being wheeled towards me, in one of the blue invalid carriages with a hood and big wheels. I had seen plenty of suffering and illness since I had arrived here but the sight of this small figure hit me across my face like a wet towel and I actually reeled backwards.

This boy was but a Belsen wraith with a thin, pointed face and a shrunken head, barely any hair, cold dead eyes and blotched skin. There was a dreadful lack of animation about every part of him to the degree that he barely seemed alive at all though it was his lower forearms and hands which caught my attention: nothing but parchment skin on bone with fingers that could only be described as tiny and skeletal. This boy was not a boy so much as a terrible disease imprisoned by a human shape and you knew – you just knew without a shadow of a doubt – that this terrible illness, perhaps AIDS, was soon going to leave him for dead.

I was still reeling from the shock of seeing him as he was pushed past me and did not even notice who was pushing him. I was focusing so powerfully on him and his shrivelled limbs that I took in nothing around him.

But, after I had calmed down, I was left with only one question: what was I feeling so sorry for myself about? I'd had a full and exciting life, three sons, a good marriage and written a few decent books. I had even planted a tree in Israel, fulfilling that ancient injunction that every man should father a son, write a book and plant a tree, and I had almost constantly roamed the world and tasted many of her greatest sights and pleasures.

Yet this lad had clearly never been offered anything except a handful of spit and a bucket of broken glass. He probably couldn't even read a book let alone write one. He would certainly never know the exquisite joys of holding a woman and would never journey much further than a sick bed and certainly not on his own. That boy was but a vegetable with no future, no present and not much of a past.

I was not to know it at that time but that Belsen wraith cured me of my own health problems. My coronary veins remain occluded but, for the rest of my pilgrimage to Compostela, I never once worried about them. The real danger with most illnesses, I have long believed, is the constant worry about them. When I lost my breath or my legs felt weak I simply stood there until my breath returned and my legs could get going again. My anxieties about my forthcoming operation disappeared and I more or less accepted that, when I dropped off my perch, I dropped off my perch, end of story. I also decided there and then never again to ask God for anything at all and to be content to receive whatever he might be gracious enough to offer me in the sunset of my years

It took maybe a day or two for the full implications of this encounter to sink in but I knew immediately, in that moment of reeling shock, that something special had happened to me here in Lourdes and I spent the rest of my time in the Domaine in an overwhelmingly good humour.

Later in the afternoon I went down to the baths just next to the grotto where queues of pilgrims were waiting to be dunked by the *brancardiers*. Prayer cards in the baths are written in 19 languages and each bath can process 85 pilgrims an hour. Early in the morning the water can be really freezing but, towards the end of the session, it gets quite warm and soupy. Around 2,500 persons are bathed here each day. They can be suffering from ailments like boils, syphilis, cancer and tuberculosis but no one has ever been infected by this water and the *brancardiers* often drink a glass of it at the end of each working day as an act of faith.

But this water must have a powerful psychological influence. John the Baptist plunged sinners into it, including Jesus himself. Water stands for the Gospel, the angels, the science of saints and the Holy Spirit. It also tells us about the resurrection and a new life. It is one of God's most primary instruments.

There are no medical staff in the baths and it is not claimed that the water has any medicinal value. These baths are purely a small surgery of hope where it is not so much the ailing body which is cured, although this may indeed happen, so much as the ailing spirit which is revived – as had happened in my case. For reasons which are still unclear to me I decided not to be bathed. I had already had my cure.

The candlelight procession and evening service that night in the Domaine was one of the most relentlessly inspiring sights under heaven. It began in the twilight with invalid youngsters again being wheeled up in lines into the quadrangle in front of the Basilica which had been lit up together with the statue of Notre Dame de Lourdes and a cross up on a nearby hill. The invalid youngsters were mostly pushed by their mothers who, heart-breakingly, all kneeled behind their carriages, mutely pleading with the Holy Mother to heal the fruit of their own wombs.

A bell rang dolefully and the sun started to sink behind the Pyrenees as thousands began gathering at the entrance to the Domaine before marching in slow and careful procession down through the trees and thickening darkness, each holding up a candle and singing the Canticle of Bernadette with each stanza ending with an *Ave Maria*. 'Immaculate Mary, our hearts are on fire . . .'

A distant jet was spearing a vapour trail across the face
of a dying sunset. A few swallows bulleted overhead looking for a late supper and, when the night had really settled
in, the Domaine looked magnificent with a moving river of
candles which caught everything in a flickering warmth.
Occasionally a charred and smokey smell wafted towards
you where a candle had burned its cardboard holder and
the whole lot had been dropped on to the ground to burn
on its own.

As the procession progressed the candles seemed to be
held ever higher and, for a moment, it was as if the whole
universe was going to burst with a spectacular and fiery cry
of sorrow. Candles are as central to the religious ritual here
as water. Their flames prolong our prayers long after we
have stopped saying them. Their incandescent purity
speaks of a holiness which is at the very heart of the
Christian Mystery. They are a massed call on the Lord
telling him that they whom he lovest are indeed sick.
Christ, the great healer, said: 'I am the light of the world.'

Now the candles were turning around and around on
themselves in huge, whirling wheels of fire and, at certain
times of the year, there can be as many as 60,000 in this
procession which lasts for up to two hours until they
gather in front of the Basilica to chant the Credo, affirming
their belief in God in Latin.

At the end of the service I hung around the grotto long
after the crowds had gone, sitting in the darkness and
feeling the undoubted power of a century of prayer. The
many huge candles lit and left here during the day by
pilgrim groups from such places as Toledo, Zagreb and
Santa Barbara, were still glowing over the jagged rocks of
the grotto, making many of the discarded crutches appear
to float in the darkness. The river was murmuring softly
behind me.

This place of candles and water, prayer and pain is valuable.

As well as brightening up wayward travellers like myself and offering solace to the suffering, it also brings the maimed and sick out into the open when our instincts are to lock them away. We are judged by the way we look after our sick. How we tend our ill reveals if we are a civilized society or not.

And as I remained there in the cold darkness I felt some of the warm pleasure of God that so many of the old and broken of his flock had made their way here in acts of faith. These invalids, with their multiple and horrific injuries and disabilities, were close to him, I decided. And they were especially close to his son who knew everything there was to know about welts of pain, the cruelty of rejection and the illnesses that destroy everything, including hope itself.

3

The Path of Love

I met my first genuine pilgrim, as he made his way along the road to Compostela, in the small French town of St-Jean-Pied-de-Port, a mile or so before the Spanish border. This frontier town has all the marvellous beauty of the ordinary although its atmosphere kept reminding me of that other famed pilgrimage centre, Canterbury, with its rackety old buildings and surprising aspects of rivers running behind the backs of houses and their tiny geranium gardens.

Fat trout swam in the river under bridges where visitors fed them with bread. Yet these crafty trout knew the difference between a nice bit of bread and the other kind with a nasty fishing hook embedded in it since they freely took the visitors' bread but I never saw anyone pull out one of them with a hook and line, although it wasn't through lack of trying. At night these same bridges became hopelessly picturesque, lit by street lamps which threw an orange glaze on the moving water as bats flew this way and that looking for food. We were in Basque country and their florid, nationalist graffiti were scrolled over many stray walls. Down in a distant valley there were eagles.

The town square was scattered about with lively bars and pizza joints where, at different times during the day, people arrived in a variety of ways – on foot, bicycle, car and even on horseback – since this is one of the main staging posts directly into Northern Spain.

In the back streets you could also buy a small passport declaring your status as a *Peregrino del Camino de Santiago*, recording the start of your journey here and with oblong spaces for the colourful and elaborate stamps for various stages of the journey such as Pamplona, Estella, Burgos and Logroño. This proves you are a true pilgrim who has followed the path of St James and which you can then show in an office in Compostela who will issue you with the all-important *compstelle*.

In another back lane I found a wooden door studded with brass scallop-shells and a bishop's palace with a small scallop prison into which they used to fling any thieves stupid enough to try and prey on passing pilgrims. This scallop motif was to be found almost everywhere I looked over the next few months – on roads, above doors, on door knockers and church bosses and on the sides of houses, all singing their little medieval songs to the passing pilgrim.

Here I also met my first walker, a tall blonde man, a lean and angular romantic with a diamond glint of intensity in his fiercely blue eyes. You knew, without him even opening his mouth, this man was born to be unhappy and, to a degree, that *had* been true, but not today and particularly not now because he had his new love, the equally tall Fenneke Veuger, walking the pilgrim path with him.

His story came out, over a few beers and a pizza in the square and, oh boy, what a lovely story it turned out to be. My new pal, Frans Van Gisbergen, was an Utrecht police-man and these Dutch bobbies clearly have longer holidays than even British schoolteachers since, so far this year, he had been walking The Road from Holland to Compostela for a little more than ten weeks.

He had begun his pilgrimage in March, he said as he devoured his pizza faster than I have ever seen a pizza devoured, although he had not been walking for any religious reasons but because a long-time girlfriend had dumped him and, demented with grief, he decided the long walk would help him sort out his feelings and even to come to terms with the loss of her. He was not clear how how this might happen but that was the plan.

After walking 300 miles or so he realized it was hopeless. She had stayed with him almost every step of the way; everywhere he looked she was there and his emotional wounds were not healing and, if anything, the loneliness of The Road was aggravating them. But he pressed on when, rather more prosaically, one of the soles fell off his walking shoes and he couldn't find another pair suitable for his outsize flat feet so he broke his journey and flew home to Utrecht where, while waiting for his new shoes to be made, he went to a party and met his new love, Fenneke, a social worker who was now sitting and smiling a lot next to him as she worked her way through her own pizza.

The point was that Frans was happy again – 'I never thought I would ever meet a girl as mad as me' – and so, fully back in the love business and with a new pair of walking shoes, he flew back to where he had broken off his walk to Compostela and set out again wearing a smile as big as the Pyrenees.

He had fully recovered from the loss of his former girl-friend but his big smile soon began wearing thin again since he was now missing his Fenneke who had to stay back in Utrecht social working. So there he was walking through the history of Europe, warm with his new love, in his new shoes and all he was doing was thinking about her, worrying where she was going at night, talking to her, wishing she was there with him. Ah yes, we all know what a smelly, inherently improbable business this game of love is.

Utrecht social workers simply do not have the holidays

of Utrecht policemen but, only two days earlier, Fenneke had joined him and he was happier than a dog rolling on his back in muck as, on their four long legs, they strode The Road together. This was it. Love was in the air. From now on they were going to stick together like Velcro. His heart was singing with her very being. They might even get married when they got to Compostela.

Frans talked a lot about his soul and, in the light of his broken shoe and the happiness it had brought him, I suggested he should perhaps write an account of his walk and love life which he could call *The Sole of my Soul*. He jumped up and down with happiness at the thought before proceeding to finish Fenneke's pizza. He could certainly eat for the Common Market but there was more flab on a butcher's bike.

He was a delight to be with and certainly one of the oddest policemen I have ever met, making me wonder how bug-eyed romantics like him manage to keep law 'n' order in Holland if indeed there is any law 'n' order in Holland. But I found the notion of The Road as the path of love extremely attractive. If I were young and wild and in love again I could think of no better way of celebrating that love than by taking her by the hand and setting out on the pilgrim road to Compostela.

It is put about that Spain has a wonderful climate with lots of bright sunshine but I've never seen any of it. The first holiday I ever took with my family, all of 30 years ago, was to Benidorm and we spent two weeks huddled together under a large beach umbrella forlornly watching the rain falling on the sea.

Only two years ago, admittedly in the middle of February, we again jumped in our camper and went looking for some

Spanish sun to cheer us up. We crossed the Bay of Biscay
in a force nine gale and, on our arrival in Santander, hail-
stones the size of golf balls came smashing down on us.
Then more snow than in the Arctic fell on everything and
we spent several days slithering this way and that in our
tiny camper, making virtually no progress. Children came
running out of schools, bursting into laughter and flinging
snowballs at us which kept going *bing, bong, bing* on the
van's aluminium walls.

The Spanish, who have grave difficulty driving properly
even when the weather is fine, were also having a terrible
time, slewing across the road, bashing into one another
and ending up nosedown in snow-filled ditches. We finally
got totally stuck in Pamplona and didn't get out again for
three days.

It wasn't exactly snowing when I left St Jean-Pied-de-Port
but the rain was bucketing down in monsoon torrents with
virtually the whole length of the Pyrenees swathed in thick
mists. Lorries came bursting out of the mists with headlamps
full on and horns blaring as I followed the twists and turns
of the long high road up the mountain. Occasionally the
mists opened up onto small wet vistas of scabby sheep foraging in sheets of cold drizzle. The rain and sheep kept
reminding me of Wales where we are all experts in wet rain
and scabby sheep. Had I wanted to soak up all this rain
and be stared at by these sheep I could easily have stayed
at home in Wales, I thought bitterly as I jerked away from
another lorry as it roared down on me out of the mists.

It surely couldn't be possible – could it? – that the
Spanish Tourist Board had simply conned the world into
believing that Spain is a land of sunshine when, in reality,
her weather is every bit as bad as that which keeps everyone's life so permanently blighted in wet and windy Wales?

There is a deeply romantic aura about the notion of pilgrimage, probably derived from medieval times, in which we pilgrims would travel from monastery to monastery where, after a hard day's walking, the monks would feed us and re-charge our spiritual batteries. This huge, stone monastery would be alive with bells and chanting and, in this holy place, we would have enduring insights into our very beings as we made our long journey through this vale of dreams and tears. After a night of light prayer and deep sleep we would set out on our way feeling wonderful. Or so the romantic concept of pilgrimage has it.

The reality is often different as I discovered when I pulled into the forecourt of the huge monastery of Roncesvalles, one of the first shelters for the pilgrim traveller in Spain, and looked up at a militaristic building with a zinc roof which reminded me of Colditz. The cafeteria was packed with pop music and singing drunks and you had to pay to get into the museum. Several charabancs pulled up with schoolchildren tumbling out clutching their overnight bags. Teachers yelled at them in the way that teachers do and the children didn't take a blind bit of notice in the way that children don't. One young girl blew a large bubble with her bubble gum which collapsed back all over her face and into one of her eyes.

Just outside the pilgrim hostel itself was a ragged line of walkers with their backpacks and walking staves scattered around them, all fagged-out and extremely miserable as you might expect after walking up some 20 almost vertical miles in the beech woods of the Pyrenees through the Roncesvalles pass. They were waiting for the hostel to open and I tried to start a conversation with a few of them but they weren't remotely interested, wanting only to take a warm shower, dry off, have some food and get their heads down on a pillow for a brief escape into a few harmless dreams. I could actually feel their aching tiredness myself and had the impression that, had I rolled up in a double-decker bus and offered to take them all home, almost the whole lot of them would have got on and told me to step on it.

A lot of them were examining their bruised, cut and blistered feet, fingering their wounds sorrowfully and wondering aloud how best to treat them. Feet were an almost constant pilgrim obsession, I was to discover over the next few months. Many of them seemed to spend more time attending to their feet than actually walking on them, fussing over them, binding them up, sticking plasters on the cuts, piercing the blisters with needles and rubbing them with secret lotions. Any real foot doctors along the *Camino* would have done a roaring trade and I was to come across a few of those. 'The first great mystery of this pilgrimage was, quite simply, Feet. Condition of,' wrote journalist Adam Hopkins in the *Daily Telegraph*.

The pass at Roncesvalles is at the centre of the lively history of this area. Numerous armies have made forays in and out of Spain through this pass and it was here where Roland and the Paladins of Charlemagne fell in a battle which was later immortalized in the *Song of Roland*.

Charlemagne led an army into Spain in 777 when he besieged a few cities before suffering after a Saxon attack and deciding to return home. As the army was retreating they were set upon by the Basques – whom Picaud had described as 'A barbarous people, full of trickery, black of colour, drunken, expert in all violence' – and who destroyed his rearguard, commanded by Roland, Lord of the Breton Marches. With all his troops lying dead all around him, Roland blew the horn of Olifant and slashed a great gap in the Pyrenees with his magic sword. Legends multiplied after this battle and the Basques became Saracens, Charlemagne became 200 years old and the battle had become an infamous example of Western Chivalry.

The monastery here was built in 1132 by the Bishop of Pamplona who was worried that so many pilgrims were falling victim to wolves and snow. Several years later the Augustinian canons made it one of the great hospitals of Christendom and until the eighteenth century it would take in travellers for three days, giving them meals, hot water and baths. Pilgrims also qualified for a free burial here as well as the services of a doctor and a cobbler. The monastery served up to 30,000 meals a year, an average of a hundred each day.

But, oh, how these pilgrims had suffered and another large fly in the pilgrim ointment here in Roncesvalles, in a manner of speaking, was even now trundling down towards them in the giant, beefy shape of Helmut, a German whom everyone tried to avoid. Once you start this pilgrimage, apparently, you tend to travel in clusters, sometimes pairing up and at others breaking away, but you keep seeing much the same walkers even if you might not see one of them for a week.

Well, Helmut was firmly lodged in this cluster, alas, and the problem was that many of the pilgrim *refugios* were small and Helmut's snores were loud. These snores were almost nuclear, one German walker said with a sorrowful shake of his head. Even after a long, exhausting day on The Road you could be woken by Helmut's snores which almost exactly replicated the start of a large earthquake. Even now I could just about see whole gangs of terrified pilgrims fleeing across the mountains of Northern Spain at top speed with their hands over their ears, hoping against hope they would never have to spend another night under the same roof as Helmut.

But here he was again, large as life and twice as nasty, a picture of bovine beefiness and you could tell, just by looking at him, there was nothing about him that could be small – especially his snores.

Well, at least I didn't have to put up with them and so I
decided to spend an hour with God in the lovely chapel
around the corner before moving on. I do this regularly on
my travels, sitting in front of the altar and trying to focus
on the meaning of what I was doing and, to be honest,
sometimes dropping the occasional, small plea that the day
might turn up a nice little story or two.

Little stories like Helmut's snoring or Frans' improbable
love life have always revived me like a nice whiff of oxygen.
They make me happy especially after wandering around all
day finding nothing. I suppose I've never been more than
just an old hack at heart; never quite come to terms with
leaving Fleet Street as it once was to take up the even absur-
der profession of writing books.

So I was just sitting there alone in the pews of the
Roncesvalles chapel and having a chat with God about my
journey so far and how the stories were flowing in nicely
and how I was thankful about that when four priests, in
black suits and dog collars, came and sat in front of me
where they took about 20 minutes going through their
Offices.

I guessed they were attached to the monastery and
thought no more about them until, around 30 minutes
later, I was driving along through the drizzling rain when I
spotted the four of them again, in two pairs, the one
behind the other, scuttling along with a military precision
like four pall-bearers who had just lost their coffin and had
to find it again pretty damned quick.

I braked and watched them continue down the road
with the two of them in the rear continually looking up
and around them in the manner of a couple inspecting a
house they were thinking of buying. But no such day-
dreaming for the two in front who were marching along
determinedly with their faces set straight ahead of them
when, as if on some pre-arranged signal, they all stopped,

put their hands together prayerfully, looked up at an old stone cross on the side of the road and began another of their long, muttering Offices. This cross dates from 1880 and is known as Roland's Cross. It replaced the ancient *Cruz de Roland*, I discovered in my guide book, which was destroyed by the French revolutionary armies in 1794 as 'tribute to the spirits of our ancestors'.

As I began to understand what was going on in front of the cross my heart clouded with delight. Here were four priests who were clearly setting out to clean up the *Camino* with their prayers; a foursome who were going to work The Road and purge it of all evil by firing off fusillades of flash prayers along the lines, perhaps, that God might hold all future pilgrims in his great and merciful hands, keeping them safe from robbers, not forgetting the multiple ailments of their sore feet.

A day which had begun for me with so much cold and miserable rain had ended in a warm splash of wonderfully golden sunlight.

4

A Bed of Beautiful Thunder

Once over the border and into Spain a series of subtle deteriorations began taking place, I wrote in my note-book. Then, after biting my lip for a while and staring at that sentence, I struck out the word *subtle* and replaced it with the words *clear* and *definite*. This was another country again and, whatever else they were, you could never accuse the Spanish of being subtle. There was probably more subtlety in a car crash than there was in the whole of Spain.

The first thing I noticed was that all their washing was hung out to dry outside the windows in their high-rise flats. Nothing wrong with that, of course, except the gendarmes would arrive by the busload if you hung out anything at all in snooty old France. Hanging out a pair of knickers to dry in Cannes was practically a hanging offence.

Then, to my extreme irritation, I discovered that most all the churches in Spain were locked when there wasn't a service in progress which put an end to a lot of my happy rummaging about in dusty ecclesiastical corners. Lots of the houses were firmly locked and shuttered too with high wire fences and huge, slavering dogs on the ends of long bits of rope. It all rather gave off the air of a criminal society. The Basque terrorists were still very much active, I was to learn, kidnapping people, bombing buildings and generally doing what terrorists do.

I was sitting in my van by the side of a yellow field of grain in the high hills of Navarre, sharing some meat and bread with six or so flies, when a Californian man wandered over to say 'Hi'. He had, he said, been walking for three days with his partner and they were now desperate to get to Pamplona to unload a lot of their gear in the Post Office. They had brought far too much with them and the excess was going to get posted back to San Diego.

Pilgrims, I was to learn, spend a lot of their time trying to lighten their loads, even to the extent of tearing the pages out of their guide books and throwing them away after they had walked that chapter. Pamplona Post Office, as one of the first proper staging posts on The Road in Spain, probably made a fortune out of sending stuff like tents back home.

These two Californians had discovered that the pilgrim *refugios* were perfectly adequate, many spotlessly clean and beautifully maintained. Only the night before they had both slept in the same bed as the actress Shirley Maclaine, that doyenne of New Agers who had done this walk three years back and had also written a best-selling book *Out Of My Body*. 'There have been many times on this walk when I wish I'd really been out of my body,' she had written with a suggestion of real pain in the *refugio*'s Visitors' Book.

The pilgrim path did not always follow the flat road, often diving off into woods and down ravines and the Californians were finding it a real problem making it through the rougher terrain where the deep pools left by the rain concealed rocks which could easily twist your ankle. You were always in danger of slipping in cow dung or getting tangled up in brambles. The path was also marked by yellow arrows on the odd rocks which became bright for a while before trailing away into faint daubs as the painter evidently ran out of enthusiasm for his work towards the end of the day.

I didn't want to spoil the integrity of their walk, I said, but they were welcome to a lift into Pamplona if they were finding their loads too heavy. The man refused my offer but his partner wasn't happy. 'Tell me what's your rationale for saying that?' she asked him in a delicious bit of California-speak. 'Come on. What's the rationale for you to say that?'

I hadn't exactly taken to Pamplona when I had slithered into it sideways in the snow a few years earlier but at least the snow had made it look neat and clean. Now the capital of Navarre looked even less enticing as I picked my way through her zooming traffic and distinctly grubby streets in the pouring rain.

Even though it was a Sunday the cathedral in the old part of the city was locked after the morning service and looked neglected with clumps of weeds growing out of the walls and roof. Right next to the cathedral was a medieval kitchen which served up food to pilgrims on their way to Compostela. The kitchen has one large open chimney surrounded by four smaller ones and the refectory has a lot of sculpted reliefs. Pilgrims would also stay in a nearby hospice which is now a museum with a plateresque facade. This means an interestingly overwrought style 'in the fashion of a silversmith', taken from Gothic, Renaissance and Moorish patterns.

The surrounding bars in the old streets pounded with disco and red-eyed drunks, all seriously refreshed after a long lunchtime session on the San Miguels. Even the dogs looked drunk as they snarled and brawled with one another in the cobbled squares.

The bull ring was as small and as empty as it was comic, something which might have been erected for a Gilbert and Sullivan opera. The bust of Ernest Hemingway – who had practically invented this place with his hairy-chested rhapsodies about bull-fighting – was spattered with pigeon droppings. You'd think they'd at least clean *him* up.

The famous San Firman festival was due to start in around two weeks' time and I was thinking of hanging on for it since the bulls running through the streets would have made some lively copy. But I quickly decided against staying for this squalid race which was hardly anything to do with a pilgrimage – no matter how widely such a venture might be defined – and anyway I had been warned that almost every thief and gangster in Spain pitched up here for the festival, robbing the tourists, often with violence.

One young Basque told me he went from Bilbao to this festival with three friends, a full wallet and a new car. He had drunk a fair bit, he admitted, but, within four days, he had lost the lot and found himself walking home to Bilbao, broke, hungover and alone.

Never a fan of Hemingway, I had also found it difficult to take bull-fighting seriously particularly after, albeit a long time ago, I had once flown to Madrid for the *Sunday Times* to interview the well-known matador Henry Higgins or El Henry as he was known to the English tabloids. He turned out to be a handsome and engaging young Londoner except it quickly emerged that his tabloid fame was totally out of proportion to his actual talent.

The Spanish bull-fight establishment were extremely reluctant to let him into their big rings where he mostly confirmed their predictions that he would get hurt. When I met him he was pretty broke and his well-worn suit of lights, some of them long extinguished, was up for sale in the hotel foyer for something like £50 o.n.o. When he could get a fight it was mostly down in the tourist rings around

Alicante or Benidorm where the bulls tended to be slower and a lot more arthritic. Yet he still managed to get some awful gorings down there even if his enthusiasm for getting impaled on a pair of sharp horns remained undimmed.

'It's the extraordinary range of emotions you feel during the day when you're fighting, from that moment of terror when you wake up feeling sick,' he told me in one of his Hemingwayesque flights of macho fantasy made all the odder by his strong Cockney accent. 'Then you meet your friends, rest before the fight, try to get a little peace; dress and there's the bull. All the time your emotions are being played on. It's like a trip. If you do it well, it keeps your spirits high for days and even if they're booing and throwing cushions into the ring, at least they're throwing them at you.'

But I could never take El Henry very seriously, particularly as he was continually trying to clip money out of me although, sadly, he was to die a few years later – not on the horns of a bull but in a water ski-ing accident.

After the wild and rainy mountains just after the border, followed by the complexity of the Pamplona traffic system – made infinitely more complex by the lack of any proper road signs which had either fallen down or were strategically hidden behind a hedge – The Road opened up high, wide and handsome onto the plains of Navarre, a flat panorama of low hills patchworked by fields of golden corn – the *meseta*.

The sun had actually come out, by way of a novel change and, in some places, these shimmering cornfields had so many red poppies on them the red had intermingled with the gold and created mauve waves which moved back and forth in the quivering sunshine and the light winds.

This was one of the most subversively beautiful landscapes I have travelled across and I kept stopping and getting out to walk around, revelling in the mauve and gold tides, the blue skyline and the stone darkness of distant mountains. The sides of The Road were spattered with a glaze of light blue cornflowers. White butterflies tumbled around these cornflowers and every stray breeze seemed to carry a new scent in its delicate hands – lavender, thyme, fresh bread, parsley and even that whiff of fresh ice cream with which I was becoming so familiar.

Behind the outlying dark hills were larger and darker mountains. Closer still were odd, small hills with whorled peaks, little more than toffee-coloured sand dunes really, a few with farmsteads on them but most of them devoid of anything except their own moon-like loneliness.

On the next high hill I stopped and watched a spread-out line of pilgrims walking The Road. There were maybe 30 of them stretched over a mile or so, striding through this sunshine morning looking like a line of worker ants as they shouldered their huge backpacks. It was at that moment that my imagination caught hold of something in the dark and instinctive forces behind a long, hard pilgrimage. Out here on the *meseta* you could walk all day and know something of your mind and your being and its totally fractional place in the mind and being of this sacred earth. Somewhere out here you could reach out and touch the hem of God as you passed him by. You could even, with a bit of luck, locate your own place in the history of the world. Lonely, mystical thoughts, I know, but pilgrimage is a lonely, mystical business.

I spotted my four priestly pall-bearers marching along in the middle of the others too, full of determination and sharply pistoning elbows. A few cars followed and a bus and more walkers, all following the long pilgrim path to Compostela.

The villages out this way were perched on the top of hills; small, sparse affairs with crooked streets joining irregular cobbled rectangles and clearly originally designed for a single donkey going one way but not two going in opposite directions. These streets and cobbled rectangles were invariably scattered around a locked church sitting directly on the hill's summit and brooding majestically over the red tiled roofs of the houses like some some giant swan watching carefully over her young.

I arrived at one such village during the afternoon *siesta* when nothing and no one moved anywhere. Dogs lay in the shade of courtyards, their sleeping muscles quivering to the touch of flies or their own anxiety dreams about heavy sticks across their rumps. A television flickered and droned to itself high in the corner of an empty bar. Flowers were ablaze with colour behind the iron railings of verandahs or in red clay pots in the courtyards. A cockerel crowed in that strange, throaty bleat, at once so full of urgency but forever reminding us of Peter's betrayal. Swallows dived and swooped around the rooftops. A faraway door opened and closed again.

Everywhere was so quiet and deserted it was as if the word had just gone out that Genghis Khan and his boys were on their way. I ghosted from courtyard to courtyard and house to house looking for, but failing to find, any life. A sleeping dog opened one eye to look at me before closing it again. I kept on thinking of myself as a returning son of the village, a man who had gone away to some foreign country to make his fortune, where he had lain in his desolate and lonely bed every night, hating every *gringo* with a real passion and sobbing himself to sleep on his pillow and dreaming of his home village only to now return, after many years of hard work, to find that everyone had gone away and not one of them – *not a single one of them* – had bothered to so much as send him a postcard telling him they were off or even where they were going.

As it turned out I couldn't bring myself to leave this ravishing landscape and, a little further along The Road and opposite a locked sanctuary, I pulled off onto a high promontory, which overlooked the *meseta* for many miles in every direction, and decided to spend the night right there.

This was one of the few times I had gone 'wild' on the trip but no one could ever have hoped for such a thunderously beautiful bedroom. The sheer peacefulness of it all was amazing and, almost for the first time since I had got to Spain, I couldn't hear a dog barking. As it was so late in the afternoon there were no pilgrims on The Road either and I sat there on my little chair outside my van all but transfixed by the scene at my feet, totally still, not even brushing the wandering flies off my hands as I watched the sun going down over the *meseta*.

Just then something small and dark began articulating itself in the brilliant clashes of a red and gold sunset. I soon realized the small dot was a cyclist, riding out of the very eye of the dying sun and freewheeling down a long, low hill in my direction as he enjoyed all the lovely exuberance of freewheeling downhill flight, made the more pleasurable since it had almost certainly been achieved after the long and painful exertion of uphill toil.

The theology of bicycling is as clear as it is balanced and exact. The pleasure you get out of it is almost directly in ratio to the pain you put in. The love you receive is equal to the love you give. A bicycle is also almost the perfect vehicle for pilgrimage since it teaches you to be at one with everything – the night and the day, the sky and the earth, the country and the city. There is no possibility of feeling doomed by alienation on a bicycle since it takes down all imprisoning walls and insists we are all only ordinary people in an ordinary world and in the shadow of one cross.

Man, who is born free, but is now imprisoned in his car, is offered the key to freedom again when he mounts a bicycle. The bike offers him an escape from the ruinous old to the exciting new and the faithful man always chooses freedom; he understands that the old dog days of sin were always a subtle and ruinous enslavement.

Lessons in humility also come strong and hard when you are astride a bike, where your only strength is your alertness, knowing that one careless motorist, in his mighty steel chariot, can crush you as flat as a pancake. Furthermore, you cannot carry many possessions on your bicycle which is a bonus since the spiritual mind understands that you will only end up being possessed by them. 'Stripped and poor and naked' you are then properly equipped for an encounter with the Lord.

The bike is also a forceful opponent of all drugs such as nicotine and alcohol, while it also tirelessly mediates the traditional Christian virtues of a fit body and clear thought. It is the vehicle by which we can start learning the purity which the Book tells us is crucial to a real faith.

The bike also has a cold, clear intelligence unsullied by modern ideas. Unlike the car, it does not maim or pollute and is the most energy-efficient machine ever, outstripping the salmon or even the dolphin. The cyclist can travel five times faster than the walker on a fifth of the power. There is even a deep mystery about how the bicycle balances upright and the scientists talk of a continual ride into a continual fall. I have always preferred the more mystical explanation of a delicate balance between a spiritual profit and a spiritual loss.

Christ chose a lowly donkey to enter Jerusalem. As befitted the son of a carpenter he always rejoiced in the lowly, the poor and the humble. When he returns – as he will because that was his most persistent and repeated promise – I have long fancied that it will happen astride a lowly bicycle.

My bicycling days were now pretty much on hold, alas,

certainly until after my operation, so all I could do was watch the man on the *meseta* with a tinge of envy as he sped past in a whoosh of tumbling sprockets and whirling Weetabix muscles.

Ah, well, maybe one day I'd be fit enough again to come back here and do the pilgrimage as it was meant to be done – on a bike and with all the wild colours of a Spanish sunset dancing over me. Maybe.

Meanwhile the darkness was falling fast and, rather like the spider, I was getting ready to withdraw into my camper for the night when the sun seemed to decide that it wasn't going to sink after all, exploding in a renewed fury of orange and gold around the outlying mountains and valleys who seemed to be busy shifting their positions as some darkened and others became ever more luminous with yellow rivers of light.

An eagle was out circling the purpling skies, taking one last look at his kingdom while he could and a couple of chattering woodpeckers went swooping past in a curious up and down flight as if they were on an invisible scenic railway. Then something truly extraordinary began taking place in the distant sunset since, as it moved again, and, as the mountains and valleys took up new positions, the gold and red light silhouetted the black shape of one of those medieval villages built around a church on a hill, underpinning it with shafts of light and making it float on a giant brilliant Indian magic carpet like some fabulous Xanadu sitting at the end of the yellow brick road.

The dazzle and vivacity of it stayed in my mind for a long time as I locked myself into my van and settled down inside my sleeping bag. But I was restless and fitful. Strange, mad images collected on the edges of my consciousness and I knew I was in for a long uneven night of almost no sleep.

The long and the short of it was I was out here, on my own, in a strange, if beautiful, wilderness and I was full of fear. And I knew where it had come from too since I had brought it with me. I was full of tension and terrors from watching too much television and too many films; from reading too many newspapers. Tonight I didn't have a big house to lock myself inside with bolts to shove into place and a burglar alarm to switch on. Not even the doors of my camper would lock properly, so what if some man with nails sticking out of his head came to get me? What if some maniac tried to stick a knife in me? Perhaps that shark would come after me again? I'd left my little chair outside the van so maybe someone would come and pinch that?

It is a strange, stomach-churning moment when you realize that, for all your fine words, you are quite as sick as the culture which produced you; this rotten culture of ours which now lies dead and done for beneath six feet of solid television. And the real challenge of this pilgrimage, perhaps, was to shake off all these petty terrors and fears by facing up to them. The real challenge was to rid myself of my black halo of fear.

My prayer life wasn't as deep and consistent as it should be. That much was clear. Yet the experience of Lourdes had been a real breakthrough – telling me that illness was as much a matter of the mind as the body – and now I had to start carrying my own candle directly into my own darkness.

And so it was I had almost my worst night's sleep of my journey in my huge and wondrous bedroom, wondering how I might purge myself of my real sickness and even if it was possible. How long did you have to stop watching television before it stopped haunting your mind? Could I stop reading newspapers and build myself a truly new world view? Was it ever possible to be really whole in a modern world?

These were all difficult, complex questions and there seemed no easy or simple answers. But at least I knew that the real pilgrimage would now begin: not just to Compostela but directly into my own darkness; not just across a beautiful Spanish landscape but also through my own mind to search for those terrors so that I could drive them out. Such a quest could surely be at the heart of a real, modern pilgrimage.

5

Mejillones with Everything

On to Puente la Reina, another major staging post on the *Camino* and with a rackety old stone bridge, first built to cope with the booming numbers of pilgrims here and described by some as the finest medieval bridge in Spain, where I leaned over the parapet for a while and watched the water flowing beneath my feet.

Pensioners like to watch the movements of waves, I have often observed, perhaps because they tell them something about the rhythms of life in their later years, but I have always enjoyed gazing at rivers and their waving weeds and the fish moving around in them. Rivers are also like humans, constantly changing their appearance and mood from the first thing in the morning until the last thing at night. The weather keeps changing the face of the river too so there is always something new or different to look for.

There was certainly something new here in Puente la Reina since I spotted a fat moving shadow and, with a *frisson* of alarm, looked up to see a huge stork powering overhead with a fish clamped in its beak. Further investigations revealed that almost every high church roof or chimney stack hereabouts had a stork's nest perched on it. They were always unfailingly amusing to look at, these birds who seemed unconcerned by everyone, with their professorial eyes and long beaks, standing on one leg and presiding over what looked like the biggest pile of wooden splinters since Noah crash-landed his ark.

But there wasn't a lot that was amusing about trying to get a suitable meal in a restaurant here since my Spanish was as non-existent as their English. Even the waiters who, you might have thought, would understand a simple request for *steak and chips* or *beans on toast*, didn't have a word – or acted as if they didn't have a word – and, increasingly, I was entering a restaurant and, if I was lucky, pointing at someone else's meal which I fancied.

Unfortunately the few diners in that one restaurant in Puente la Reina weren't eating anything I wanted so I took hold of the menu with great confidence and ordered something, in what I hoped was a Spanish accent, but without a clue what it was. Around half an hour later I received a sort of soup of sausages boiled in sauerkraut – or it may have been the other way around – which smelt and looked so foul I half-expected the head of a little monster with drooping antennae and goggling eyes to come bobbing up out of it at any moment.

All I really wanted was a nice fat steak with lots of chips and all I ever got were these huge stews with 'strange' things in them. I did once order something which seemed vaguely familiar since it had the word *bacon* in it and, when the waiter put it down in front of me, he became extremely alarmed when I stood up and raised a clenched fist shouting 'Yes'. More by luck than design, I had ordered a lovely plate of eggs, bacon and chips which were as enjoyable as anything I have ever eaten in any Spanish restaurant.

Yet all these strange stews wouldn't have been so bad if the Spanish restaurateurs didn't seem to feel the need to have music playing and the television blaring without a break or any sort of remission for good behaviour. There's only so much football I can take on fuzzy screens, to the accompaniment of an accordion, as I pick my way through a stew whose ingredients I could barely guess at. There's also a certain predictable relentlessness about Spanish football which seems to consist of the occasional brilliant solo attack by a forward who flings himself into the air faking serious injuries whenever anyone gets within ten yards of him. But mostly it is the same boring story of stoic lines of defenders who ploddingly and efficiently repel any ball that comes their way.

Yet there were lots of pilgrims thronging these old stone streets and, on one corner, I met Sophie and Thyss, an elderly Dutch couple who were cycling to Compostela. Sophie was extremely lithe, as you might expect of an aerobics teacher, and Thyss was a huge bear of a man, an engineer who was due to retire in a couple of months. They were certainly very fit even if, at the end of each day in the saddle, Sophie smoked like a chimney and Thyss drank like a fish. I was to bump into them a lot over the next month or so on various camp sites and it was always much the same picture of them both sitting outside their little blue tent with Sophie, fag in mouth, cooking and Thyss busily trying to open another carton of wine. They say drink and cigarettes are bad for you but it didn't seem to have done them any harm.

Thyss said that he was interested in European culture and this was his way of learning it on the hoof, so to speak. Sophie just enjoyed cycling – 'I could get on a bike and cycle forever' – and the two of them were as happy a couple as I am ever likely to meet, chatting with one another all day long which is always a sign of a good marriage at a time when many couples seem to have given up talking to one another altogether, communicating by sign language in front of their television.

I always questioned the pilgrims I met about their motives for doing this pilgrimage and, thus far, had only met a few who had offered any formal religious reasons. Many seemed to have no real concept of sin or penitence and, if they did, didn't worry about it. Adventure was the main reason they offered; an unusual way of having a holiday.

It was just after midday and I was sitting quietly under a tree in a sunshine plaza next to the Cathedral de Santa Maria le Redonda in Logroño. High on her two ornamental spires were the huge, ragged nests of many storks who had virtually colonized these holy rooftops and were now making clucking sounds, a bit like hollow bamboo sticks being knocked together.

Most of the big florid porchway of the cathedral had been taken over by pigeons and occasionally there was the recorded sound of a bang, as in gun, from one of the public loudspeakers which sent the pigeons wheeling around the square in circling flights of fluttering panic. These bangs did not disturb the storks in the slightest as they remained motionless in their ecclesiastical eyries, only leaving for a spot of angling in the local river Ebro. There are about two hundred of these storks dotted about the high points of the city and although they used to leave for the sunnier climes of Africa in October, to return the following March, they had, for the last three years, gone nowhere at all, preferring to stay put here in good old Logroño.

And so, given that the city skies were also alive with the whistling whirls of many swallows, it added up to a bit of a bird problem and, as I sat there in the plaza, I might even have been sitting inside the Snowdon aviary in London Zoo except that this one was bigger, more beautiful and a lot more interesting.

Behind me a radio was blaring with a woman singing one of those fervent, buttock-clenching solos for which the sentimental Spanish have such a weakness. A group of children were playing football up against the high, wrought-iron gates of the cathedral and, just above them, was an inscription to General Franco which had apparently been too difficult to erase after the great dictator had fallen from favour. This cathedral was clearly in a real mess with cracks running up and down her walls of such earthquake proportions they would have given any normal house surveyor an immediate heart attack. The cracks had been filled in with some sort of tar and the air of general dereliction about the place wasn't much helped by the droppings of the storks.

And we are not talking tiny spatterings of swallows here, nor even of the rather larger droppings of the pigeons. We are talking whole, smelly pizzas of the stuff, full of fish bones and suspicious black lumps.

Two elderly women crossed the plaza with one holding a nine-year-old child by the hand. The women were arguing loudly – or they might have been simply discussing something with the usual Spanish animation – when the child, who was chewing gum, broke into their argument with a comment. The woman holding the child unlocked her hand from his and smacked him so hard between the shoulder blades his chewing gum shot out of his mouth. The child immediately knelt down to pick up the gum and pop it back into his mouth while his attacker, unconcernedly and barely without breaking her step, returned to her argument with the other woman.

Some of these elderly Spanish women had a certain casual cruelty about them which I found quite frightening. They went to the bullfights like ours go to bingo and I guessed they all still had photographs of Franco on walls of their living rooms. They also had a real fondness for imitation gilt jewelry, ate horses, cooked everything in mountains of garlic, put lipstick on as with a trowel and were clearly keen on fur coats. They all seemed to smoke too, had arms like Sumo wrestlers and, whenever one hove

into my direction, I quietly quailed, ready to do anything
they might ask.

There is a fascinating clutch of small churches around
the cathedral and they weren't locked by way of a refreshing
change, even if you had to negotiate a delicate passage
through at least three or four beggars who were always
thronging around the porches. I had also managed to catch
the midday communion service in the cathedral of the
storks where we each received a wafer but no wine since the
priest just stood there and drank the lot.

But, as you wandered around inside the cathedral, you
really could feel yourself brushing through the thickets of
centuries of prayer. People were kneeling in the ornate
wooden confessional boxes with their words quite audible
to anyone standing nearby. My mind always seemed to fall
out of gear a bit when I came near a confessional, trying
to come to terms with the non-stop blizzard of sin and guilt
which must have blown through those small wooden
grilles over the years. Even more mind-boggling was what
those poor old priests must have had to endure over the
years in them. It's little wonder so many of them have
turned to drink as I had discovered for myself in my years
with Alcoholics Anonymous where, if a man wasn't in
Equity, he was probably a priest . . .

The various sumptuous chapels inside the cathedral were
protected by thick iron gates and, directly behind the
main altar, I found a small painting of the Crucifixion, said
to be by Michelangelo, and embedded in a safe and with
enough wires and locks and bolts all around it to do justice
to Fort Knox. One dirty finger on that plate glass and you
just knew almost every alarm bell in Northern Spain would
start ringing.

The hollow bamboo sounds of those storks again. Another
loud bang and another wheeling flight by the briefly terrified pigeons. A shrieking squadron of swallows. I had met

an English teacher in the street, Simon Ryan, who had told me that a few years back the priests had argued that the storks were ruining the cathedral, dropping their mess on people on their way to worship and generally clogging up the gutters and fouling up the roof.

When the storks had flown off for their winter break in Africa they at least had a chance to push the nests off the roof but, now the storks were staying put – probably to keep a watchful eye on their nests after such clerical vandalism while they were away – the problem with the storks and their baby young was getting worse. In consequence the priests were calling for a full cull of the storks, Simon said. The outrage at this suggestion was unconfined and the local radicals began calling for a full cull of the priests. Storks were very rare but there had always been too many priests, ran the radical argument. Let's thin out the priests.

The radical argument did not prevail and the priests remained unculled. They do occasionally shoot the storks, when they think no one is looking but, for the most part, the storks remain unmolested, still snootily gazing down on us all when they are not actually standing up and stretching out their great wings.

A hippy came and sat next to me under the tree, muttering evilly to himself as he tried to hand-roll a cigarette with fingers shaking alarmingly. A few German cyclists had turned up and were eating their sandwiches on a bench. Another small group of walkers flopped down in the shade with their knapsacks next to them, a few taking off their shoes and examining their feet worriedly while others went to the fountain to throw some cold water over their faces.

The walkers and cyclists had obviously met one another before an.d quite a few gave me a wave or nod since I too had become a part of the fixtures and fittings of The Road, often stopping to give a walker a cup of tea while I carefully and quietly relieved him of what he knew. (I am one of those hit-and-run interviewers; painlessly in and out with my questions, with no hint of pencil or notebook, before you have barely worked out what's going on.)

It is believed almost all the million or so pilgrims to Compostela come through this square throughout the year and a lot of them arrive in an extremely rough condition. The dry, hot country starts in earnest after Puente de la Reine and they can get literally cooked. *Gambas* or prawns, the Spanish call them – on account of their red faces. They can come in here staggering all over the place or seeing double as if they had just come to the end of a gruelling marathon. One Frenchman turned up here with almost all his skin having fallen off his forehead before being taken to hospital.

There's another hazard for pilgrims here too, in the shape of a small brothel just around the corner, where prostitutes hang off a verandah touting for trade just opposite one of the small churches. But there again prostitutes have always hung around pilgrimage centres despite all the best efforts of the authorities to shoo them away. Prostitutes have always fed off the humanity and weakness of pilgrims who, to be sure, are every bit as human and weak as everyone else.

The small art museum in Logroño was suspiciously welcoming, not charging anything for admission and with an attendant actually shaking my hand – *shaking my hand!* – and smiling a lot as he explained what I might find and on what floor.

Cynicism is something that develops quite naturally on The Road since, holy path or not, you are almost constantly besieged by someone who has thought of some ruse or other to relieve you of your money. Everyone always charges something or other – even if it is only to invite a donation for a really vague, if not actually invisible service – although the charges are not exactly extortionate. It was always assumed that pilgrims were fairly broke, which was why they were suffering on pilgrimages and not sunning themselves in a Club Med, so the prices for most everything were always quite modest. You did, however, often get the feeling you were constantly being nibbled at by lots of small fish; not actually attacked but nibbled at, continually and remorselessly, from the moment you opened your eyes to that divine moment when you put your little head down on your pillow late at night. It was almost impossible to spend nothing – no matter where you were or what you were doing – although you did sometimes encounter a shark, usually in a garage, who took a really big and nasty bite out of you and your credit card, an event which could often put me in a really bad mood for hours. The trouble with such sharks is that they destroy all your plans and you end up going home sooner than expected.

But the *peregrino* was generally treated with kindness and even respect outside the normal commercial alleyways with feet tended to and advice given freely, like now, in this small museum in Logroño which hadn't even tried the smallest tickle on my rapidly dwindling supply of pesetas.

As it turned out, they might have had trouble getting the punters in here at gun-point since there were no Andy Warhols or Picassos on display although there was quite a lot of religious art. It was all highly idealized medieval stuff with paintings of Christ in Gethsemane or floating above the Mount of Olives or on the Cross. Botticelli cherubs flew around and around with glittering swords and bright, red rivers of blood poured from every wound. Christ was also frequently shown as a baby with brilliantly back-lit golden curls.

There was never any sign of any personality in the faces

either – as you always find in, say, Rembrandt – with
everyone looking pretty much as wooden as everyone else
and in a way, presumably, the original artist *thought* was
beautiful.

I have a lot of problems with the persistent sentimentality
of this kind of art which takes its subject only to drape it
in various, multicoloured drapes of pure goo. Everything
in this field of art is fake; we are here in Disneyland; a place
of empty and vulgar illusions where every feature must
glitter or wink or glow in the dark like all that rubbish piled
high in those monstrous shops in Lourdes.

This glutinous holy treacle often spreads across religious
writing too where it is often impossible to find simple and
direct writing on any issue. Meaningless phrases are piled
on top of yet more meaningless phrases in this kind of
writing and, while they might have some meaning on their
own, they have none when joined together. Every sentence
becomes a sort of mini-sermon in which we are urged to do
something or other so that we might make a swift entry into
Heaven or, unless we watch it, an even faster descent into
Hell. The authority of the Holy Mother or the Scriptures
are invoked in every other line as we are dragged, screaming
and shouting, into 'The Concert of Creation, the Cosmic
Promise of the Lord, the Franciscan adoration of the
Divine Majesty'. (Sample taken from my guide book to
Lourdes but what does it mean? Just what does any of it
mean?)

The real trouble with this meaningless writing is that it
alienates normal people in the same way as seeing a painting
of an idealized Christ with sunshine burnishing his piles
of golden curls can only make any reasonably intelligent
person totally depressed, if not actually quite ill.

This impenetrable piety is the enemy of a real Christ as
he continues moving through his real world and, standing in
that small museum in Logroño, I longed to see a painting

of a real man doing real things in this real world. I wanted
to see a painting of a man with torn clothes and work-
ripped hands; a man with a knowingness in his eyes who
knew everything about the slippery, deceptive ways of evil;
a street-wise man who spent much of his time with Pharisees
as they tried to con him; a man of invincible courage and
a violent bad temper who kicked over the tables of those
hucksters in the Temple; a man, perhaps, with trouble with
the bunions of his feet and the arthritis in his fingers; a
man who knew all there was to know about pain and who
would also have often felt the cold hands of fear gripping
his heart as he wondered what a corrupt and depraved
world was next going to dump on his head.

I longed to see a painting of a real man who would be
real to all of us forever; a man whom we might find outside
the Job Centre chatting with the poor and unemployed or
in the hospital wards holding the hands of those suffering
from AIDS without talking to them in holy jargon; a man
whom we might also find on the football terraces, as vocal
and passionate as everyone else as he cheered on his
favourite team – as long as it was *not* Manchester United.

What I did not want to look at was this dreary sentimental rubbish, tricked out in phoney sunlight and Disneyland
gilt with lashings of bright red blood everywhere, which
said nothing important to anyone and, on the contrary,
generally convinced most normal educated people that, if
this is what religion was about, then they wouldn't want to
have anything to do with it.

On reflection I'm glad I didn't pay to go into that museum when I went in and I'm glad the attendant gave me a
good smiling at and a handshake since, had I parted with
the usual pile of pesetas, I would, as sure as duck eggs is
duck eggs, have been asking for a full refund on my way
out.

Yet I do not spend much of my time foaming at the mouth

in art museums, nor do I often run away from elderly Spanish women in terror since I was now actively enjoying my pilgrimage, becoming more and more accustomed to the Spanish and even becoming fond of a few of them. They always responded warmly when I tried a bit of Spanish on them, I had discovered, prepared to then make an effort with me rather than before when I merely waved my hands around uselessly. I had never found this quality of friendliness in the French who always seemed to sneer at or patronise you no matter what efforts you made or how good your French might be.

I was certainly enjoying many of the municipal camp sites in Spain where I could often park up next to a river or overlooking a lake for around £4 a night. Some prefer to 'wild' camp and this is perfectly possible almost anywhere in Spain, providing you tuck yourself out of the way. I was now 'wilding' about twice a week if – and only if – I saw somewhere really inviting. But, generally, I was more than happy to spend the £4 for a good spot on a proper site, often with a supermarket, a bar, congenial company and the use of their lavatories and showers.

The standard of the lavatories was invariably high and here in Logroño, in the Camping La Playa, the showers and lavatory were almost like one of those modern churches with a polished tiled floor, piped music, stained glass windows and vases full of fresh flowers. In fact it was all so lovely and clean I took one look around as I walked into it with my toilet things and walked out again thinking I had gone into the wrong place.

Also, if the sun is up in the morning, there is really no nicer way of starting the day than by making yourself a nice mug of tea and sitting on a chair outside your camper, sipping your tea as you watch the morning come together. It is certainly unfailingly better – even when it is pouring down with rain – than being in some stuffy hotel where, more often than not, you have been kept awake by the thump of a disco of a wedding party until the early hours or, much worse than that, the noises of a drunken couple arguing or fighting or doing whatever in the next bedroom which always seems to have wafer-thin walls.

You also, in a camper van, don't feel obliged to tackle some enormous greasy breakfast, swimming in puddles of fat, simply because you have paid for it. I've had long mornings of heartburns without number because I've felt I had to at least try the hotel breakfast and always regretted it.

You don't have to call for a stretcher party for your credit card on a camp site either as you often do at a hotel reception desk by the time they have added on the service charges for the service you can never remember receiving, the drinks you can never remember drinking and the charges for the telephone calls you can never remember making. But there is no forgetting this rapidly inflating bill which all then comes at a standard rate of VAT.

Sophie and Thyss had found they were often not allowed to sleep with one another in the *refugios* so they had tried a small hotel a few times on this trip when the weather had got really bad and had always regretted it. A huge Danish drunk had burst into their bedroom in the middle of the night. In another hotel a man's industrial-strength snoring in the next room – Helmut again? – had all but blasted them out of their bed. From now on they were going to stick to their blue little tent and one another, no matter how bad the weather got.

Being so useless at translating Spanish menus I had also ended up buying most of my food in the supermarkets where, invariably, they had little *photographs* on the tins of what they had inside them. A sausage looks like a sausage in any language, after all. It is impossible to mishear a tin of beans. A pea is a pea is a pea. You can even, if you read the small print, usually find the contents *written in English.* And so it was that I developed an absolute passion for *mejillones,* Spanish mussels which I had on just about everything – even toast. From now on the journey was – to paraphrase the title of Arnold Wesker's play – *Mejillones with Everything.*

Buying my own stuff also meant I could maintain a fairly sterile food system and, almost for the first time for many years, my travels were not interrupted by the runs which they have been, times without number, whenever I've been eating exclusively in restaurants, many of which, I have long suspected, never throw out anything – even if it had gone rotten or mouldy when they merely throw it in the curry.

The savings of cooking for yourself are also enormous, of course, particularly when you drink as much tea as I do. It is difficult to get a pot of tea these days – even in the most modest restaurant – for anything less than a pound. Take a biscuit or a small cake and the price goes ballistic. So, for me, boiling my own kettle for my tea was an immediate saving of at least a fiver a day and I always kept my fridge stocked with soft drinks since most restaurants out these ways will charge £2 or even £3 for a small Fanta and not even have the decency to blush with embarrassment when they do so. If only I could have found a cheap substitute for petrol I really would have been in holiday heaven.

It is not exactly paradise on four wheels, however, as I discovered on my last night in Logroño when I awoke with a start, sweat bubbling on my forehead and eyes so wide I might have been in a ghost house. Right here in the darkness was the whine of a marauding mosquito, travelling from my left ear to my right and back again like some stray stereo effect.

The point is I hadn't slept with my van windows open since that mosquito had got me on the nose way back in

France. So what did this mean? Had one somehow got in or did I have a stowaway mosquito on board? I checked that my windows were closed and concluded I did indeed have a stowaway in the van who had probably helped himself to the blood in my poor nose and then fallen asleep in some dark corner only to wake up a few weeks later and was now about to help himself to another belly-full.

So it was action stations again, the light on and the can of Raid at the ready except, naturally, he had immediately scarpered and could have been almost anywhere. A little later I was lying in the darkness when that unmistakable stereo of a whine returned followed by the dive-bombing bit and an equally unmistakable bite on my left shoulder.

More action stations but it was useless. He had clearly got my blood and was already happily tucked up in his secret bed and sleeping it off. Ah well. If indeed he'd had his fill then maybe I wouldn't hear from him for another two weeks. After again checking that my van windows were closed I rolled over and fell into a sort of sleep.

6

The Battle of the Wine

Black rain clouds began building into shapeless, frothy castles on the skyline as I left Logroño to poke around the region of Rioja where, as befits a world-famous wine centre, the vineyards stretched right out to those shapeless, becastled horizons. Here again there was none of the orderly prissiness of France and I kept coming across rackety smallholdings with makeshift fences and little squares of corn, beans and potatoes with, here and there, a line of gladioli doing nothing else but lining up in their gaudy colours looking raggedly vulgar.

Those lovely marigolds also kept popping their black, moon faces up out the squares of corn. Some of the larger cornfields had already been harvested and the farmers had been burning the stubble, sending uneven drifts of smoke chasing one another across the fields. But, even with the rain threatening, I loved being back in the vineyards, often pulling up to spend an hour wandering down their serried ranks with the small bunches of grapes hiding shyly underneath the leaves somewhere around my knees. Everything was being brought to a whistling perfection and soon they would begin picking these grapes.

The mood of these Rioja vineyards was almost mystical and wandering through them was often like walking across the altar of the world. Stand alone on one of these strange, sultry mornings, raise up your arms and close your eyes. You can smell the land and taste it and feel the life powering up out of the earth. Kneel in the singing soil and pick a bunch of young grapes. Hold this bunch in both your hands and you will understand why grapes have always been so revered throughout history; why they are always so central to the Christian Mystery and why there is always the image of the grape in serious, devoted societies. If a vine is cut at a certain time of year it can bleed to death.

The vine features prominently in Christ's teaching and he referred to himself as the Blood of the Covenant. He turned water into the finest wine at the wedding at Cana and, when it ran out, he made some more. This act has been taken to foreshadow the Eucharist when we are asked to drink the wine in remembrance of him. So the wine also becomes the very blood of the earth and we can think of it as Christ's blood surging annually through the vineyards of the world as we commemorate the feeding of the five thousand.

This is an attractive and moving concept particularly when we try and imagine the spirit of Christ inhabiting every square inch of the earth, endowing it with the life which enables all growth.

So, still kneeling in this vineyard, squeeze your bunch of grapes and watch the luxuriant blood run in warm rivers through your fingers and across your wrists and up your arms. Smell the warmth and humanity of the juice. Let its redness astonish your eyes. Hold it up and allow the blood to trickle down into your open mouth. Feel it run along the back of your throat. Yes. Yes. This is indeed the blood of life as you kneel here at the communion rail of the altar of the world.

Rain, thunder and lightning were battling it out at the same time when I got to Haro, a working town about 20 miles north west of Logroño. It looked a lively, if crumbling place as, like everyone else, I worked my way from doorway to doorway in between the furious showers of rain. The showers stopped and started again but at least they gave you some chance to study these amazing doorways which, particularly in the old part of town, were strikingly individual and set at the wonkiest angles. The wooden doors were drilled by more woodworm than the rafters of your average English church and some of these woodworm must have been the size of a prize cucumber, judging by one hole I found. These doors certainly wouldn't have put up much resistance to any determined burglar, particularly if he was on the skinny side.

More rain, thunder and lightning. People stepped out of the porchways, held out their hands and stepped back in again. The faces in the windows went all runny and featureless. A man with a large white napkin stuffed into his collar was forking down some food. Church bells clanged. Another pause and another holding out of hands. But no. Not just yet. Time for more rain in case you didn't get wet enough the last time. It stopped again. It started again. I shared a porchway with a cat who looked up at me before we both stood there looking out into the rain.

When it seemed as if it really was going to rain forever, it stopped and the clouds cleared in a way that suggested it might stay stopped and I made my way towards the square. This weekend was a time of fiesta for Haro and these people were determined to fiesta no matter what. The band was climbing back up onto the bandstand in the Plaza de la Paz and there was toy car racing in another corner. A flamenco dancer began waving her billowing skirts about and the band struck up a tune. Young drunken boys with *botas* or wineskins slung over their shoulders stood in doorways, squirting streams of wine into their mouths from their *botas* at arm's length, doubtless trying to impress the largely indifferent girls.

They had also heated up a stew in one of the colonnades in what must have been the biggest stew-pot in the world, doling it out in polythene beakers which, with a lump of bread and a soft drink, came to a reasonable 100 pesetas – less than 50p. Mine contained an exploded sausage, a few potatoes, something green that was masquerading as a sprout and an extremely chewy bit of black meat which could easily have been sliced off the tyre of a long-distance lorry.

I found a dry corner in the square and was quietly persevering with my lorry tyre when the rain bucketed down again, stopping the band in full trumpet, putting an end to the motor racing and flamenco dancing, tipping down the gutters and out of the rain-pipes, cleansing the pavements for the fortieth time that morning and washing away the whole fiesta as everyone hurried for shelter.

Yet all this rain was doing the bars no harm, most of them now full to bursting with drunks who were going to carry on partying until they were partied out, no matter how bad the weather got. Wet outside and wet inside, one might have said. But he didn't.

They also had a bullfight on that night and, oh may God have mercy on my soul, I had bought a ticket for it. Oh look, I'm writing about Spain. Look, everyone else is going and me boycotting it was hardly going to make any difference. Look, how can I condemn something when my only experience of bullfighting has been meeting Henry Higgins holding out his hand so that I would put money in it?

But, as the hour approached and I was getting sick with worry and guilt about what I had done, this last downpour of rain clearly decided to turn itself into an hour of rain followed by another hour and yet another. Then, doubtless because all the cissy matadors were worried about getting their precious suits of lights wet, the bullfight was cancelled. Not postponed. *Cancelled.* Oh thank you God. Thank you. Thank you. Thank you.

The next morning they had scheduled an even weirder bit of Spanish madness since the annual Battle of the Wine was due to take place in a wood on an outlying hill and I had come here hoping to be in the thick of it. This was an important festival, I had been told, which both celebrated the grape harvest and ancient disputes over boundaries. These rites had sprung up all over Spain and they were always opened by a religious service.

There was one town where they drummed all weekend and yet another where they pelted one another with rotten tomatoes. I have now been to a few of these festivals and strongly suspect that, no matter what they are alleged to be about and no matter how many religious services they may have to open them, the truth is they are really only lame Spanish excuses to make a lot of noise and get hog-whimperingly drunk.

The day began promisingly enough with the sun climbing high into a blue sky and the sound of guns. I had been warned to put on some old clothes and duly set off in my camper, turning left out of the camp site and joining a scene straight out of *Mad Max*. The cars were eccentric jumbles of this and that, most of them without roofs and with exploding exhausts. A lot of their bonnets had also gone missing with the engines visible, and flags and streamers flying in their wakes. Not one of those cars would have passed an MOT in a thousand years and some of their undercarriages were actually dragging along the road in showers of sparks, not helped by the fact that they were all piled high with people, all wearing red Basque neckerchiefs and who, if it wasn't so early in the day, I would have sworn were hog-whimperingly drunk already.

Tractors were also pulling trailers decked out with vines

and yet more yelling drunks who, come to think of it, had probably just kept on going from the night before. More lorries followed loaded with huge casks of wine and then came more Mad Max cars with their horns blaring, music turned up to full blast and everyone hollering with happiness. Many kept waving at me to join in the fun. I was going to enjoy this well enough. This was going to be one great party and it had been a long, long time since I had been to one great party.

So, with one foot stuck well down on the accelerator, I slipped an Oasis tape into my cassette, gave it plenty of volume and joined the race through the countryside. I was sure it was going to be great fun when I must have got carried away with the raucous exuberance of Oasis since I missed the turn everyone else had taken. Then, as soon as I realized my mistake, I tried to do a three-point turn in an extremely narrow lane and ended up with my two front wheels stuck down a concealed drainage ditch from which I could not reverse out. I was well and truly stuck. Stuck, stuck, stuck. Liam was still blasting on about how, tonight, he was a rock 'n' roll star. Well, he could shut up for a start and I gave the eject button a good punch which hurt my hand.

The thing about getting stuck in a ditch is that you are always certain you are going to stay stuck there forever. My stupidity at taking the wrong turning was also compounded by the fact that there was no one else coming this way and all I could do was sit there as everyone else made their way to what was probably the greatest party in the whole history of Spain.

Oh, how I hated these rotten, bulky camper vans which were forever clogging up the roads and stopping everyone getting to wherever they wanted to go. They were so ugly too and, if I'd been on foot or on a bicycle – like every other self-respecting pilgrim on the road to Compostela – I wouldn't have been in this mess. I got out and aimed a kick at the back wheel which had risen a few inches off the road. The chassis had probably got cracked and I was sure to be heading for a bill of at least £500 – if I was lucky.

After about ten minutes a young lad came walking up the road eating a loaf of bread. He had an intense, oddly handsome face with long black corkscrew curls. But he was clearly as mad as a lorry since, when he wasn't chewing his bread, he was talking to himself loudly. At first he offered me a bit of his bread and, when I refused, he weighed up the situation *vis-à-vis* my stuck camper and began talking in Spanish and wouldn't stop. 'No comprendo,' I kept saying but that didn't make any difference. On and on he went, like the fabled drip, drip of the Chinese water torture, presumably giving me advice on what I must do next but, as I couldn't understand one single word, I kept shrugging my shoulders idiotically and wishing he would just go away.

But he would not shut up or go away and, by now, he could have been giving me a lecture on the ins or outs of the Spanish Civil War – or even be making a bid for the leadership of the Tory Party here in Rioja – but what I did understand for sure was that he was beginning to get on my already frayed nerves and, rather rudely, I tried to shoo him away with my hands.

That didn't stop his speechifying either and he was still occasionally offering me a bite on his loaf when he spotted a small Clio car, loaded with adults and kids, coming in our direction and I was appalled when he flagged it down and asked the driver to pull me out. A *Clio!*

The Clio driver gave me a long lecture in Spanish, of which I again did not understand one single word, presumably on how I should take more care when three-point turning out this neck of the woods. His fat wife, who was holding a small baby to her bosom, got out of her side of the car and chipped in with her analysis of the situation.

By now the three of them were talking to me and apparently in a right old paddy about my useless driving. In fact it was rather like some uproar from the Spanish delegation in the United Nations after President Clinton had announced that he was about to drop a nuclear bomb on Madrid. And all these speeches in torrents of barbed Spanish were being directed at me without any benefit of a translation service so, whatever the motion was, there was no chance I was going to have the opportunity to move an amendment to it.

The argument seemed to be emerging that I deserved all I got because I'd been so cravenly stupid as to drive my dirty old German camper into one of their lovely Spanish drainage ditches. I mean to say, there it was, this drainage ditch, the greatest jewel in the Rioja crown, their one and only award-winning tourist attraction and I'd gone and fouled the thing up by getting my camper stuck in it. Now it was going to lose all its AA stars for certain. The RAC was going to strike it out of all their guide books. Tourists would never come and look at it ever again.

Well, I hardly drove into your poxy drainage ditch on purpose, I would have said if I could have but couldn't. And anyway if they cut the grass verges around here properly then we'd see there was a ditch *there*, wouldn't we? We'd all have a bit of a chance, wouldn't we?

But I didn't say one word, of course and, when the baby started crying as well, doubtless upset by all this gabbling racket, I merely walked away from them, feeling mad and indeed looking mad since I too was now flinging my hands into the air and muttering to myself.

I was still talking to myself when the Civil Guard pulled up next to me and, without so much as one word of Spanish retribution or mention of a fat fine for careless driving, took me back to that dreaded ditch where their van winched out my van so that I could get back to the party.

By now I had missed the opening service and had to park miles away from the actual area of the Battle of the Wine since the roads leading to it were jammed. So I had to slog up a long hill on my own two feet and, very soon, the point of the event became clear when a child leaped out in front of me with an enormous Space Age water pistol and gave me a good squirt of red wine right in the face. Oh, this was shaping up into a truly wonderful morning this was.

A couple walked past me absolutely soaked with red wine – and looking none too happy about it – when another youngster leaped from behind a tree and gave me another good squirt over my trousers. Soon the crowds thickened considerably and I saw a lot of them had industrial sprays on their backs with the canisters full of red wine. These sprays were attached to guns which showered everyone in sight and, by now, I was being sprayed almost every foot of the way. Some of the young men had even set up road blocks at which you were sprayed from head to toe, particularly the young girls who yelled and screamed at the discomfort of it all. A band was playing somewhere in the distance.

By the time I had got to the centre of the action in a woodland I had been smothered with so much wine I could have poured myself into a glass and drunk myself. The sticky red stuff, which tasted awful and was certainly like nothing I had ever bought at Oddbins, was dripping off my every nook and cranny while hands had even reached out and pulled back my trousers an inch or so before squirting sprays right down my backside.

Everyone was at it – kids, old ladies, grown men, all firing off so much wine at me my shoes were squelching and I was even having difficulty in seeing properly since it was getting into my eyes. Often I took two steps forward and three back as I ran into a solid wall of squirting wine.

These vinous gun men never showed any mercy since, whenever I was standing there squeezing the wine out of my eyes and trying to wipe them dry with the tips of my fingers, they blasted me in the face again. Another spray went down the back of my trousers and another hit me on the side of the neck. We could have been in Sam Peckinpah's *The Wild Bunch* with spurts of blood flying everywhere and bodies tumbling one way and another except this bunch were clearly far wilder – and drunker – than Sam's bunch.

This wine, I soon worked out, was brought in by trailer in huge casks from the local vineyards. So, when your wine ran out, you could fill your canister or water pistol or whatever at these casks before returning to the fray. The veterans of this battle, I noticed, wore goggles and crash helmets and polythene protective clothes and, as I got squirted a few more times, with my clothes a bright red and hair matted into sticky clumps, I found myself hating them with a quiet vehemence. Why did they wear protective clothing? Why didn't they just join in the fray and *suffer* like everyone else?

I finally got to a clearing where a silver brass band was playing merrily and hundreds of people were dancing around it. Yet this dance was like no other since everyone was leaping around in a thick rain of red wine. Men with industrial sprays were standing there and squirting it up into the air, turning the whole clearing into a throbbing, heaving sea of sodden pink bodies. Even the mud they were dancing in was a bright red and presumably you could just fall over drunk and drink one of those puddles which would make you feel even drunker. A lot were, in fact, drinking the wine as well as dancing in it, all totally and obliviously happy despite the fact that it wasn't even yet 11 o'clock in the morning.

The sheer child-like daftness of the event reminded me of the night I was in Jerusalem with my friend, the poet Stewart Henderson, on Independence Day and everyone, including grown men and women, went around hitting one another on the heads with little plastic hammers that squeaked. *The Jerusalem Post* was forever writing furious editorials urging that this childish practice should stop but it never did.

The band was still giving it a lot of welly and the red rain kept raining as I stood quietly under a tree soaked in wine when some joker, whose face I never did see, crept up behind me and emptied a whole bucket of the stuff over my head. It was a truly awful experience and it succeeded in making me very cold since the sun had disappeared and those dark rain clouds were mustering again.

Nevertheless I remained standing there like a big red drip until the band stopped playing and we began squelching back to our cars, lots of us shivering and chattering with the cold. You could also tell a fair few of us, particularly the children, had long stopped seeing the funny side of it and there were even some angry words when some latecomers wanted to start spraying a few who had been sprayed enough and just wanted to get on home.

It had certainly been the oddest party and at least I had a change of clothes in my lovely camper and could also brew up a cup of warming tea. Oh how I loved my camper, I thought as, dry and warm, I drove back to Haro, past hundreds of them walking back to the town disconsolately, their clothes sopping and holding out their arms wide like bedraggled lines of gooney birds waddling home after some wild red paint party which had got out of control.

You could see the numbers of the pilgrims swelling almost daily on The Road through Rioja, all of them still carrying backpacks almost as big as themselves – a group of ten here, two there, up to fifteen in the distance – making their ways along the path through the vineyards which in

themselves had a holy atmosphere about them appropriate
to a holy pilgrimage.

But, after the raucousness of Haro, I needed some time
on my own again, a few days of silence, and so I went to
the nearby monastery at San Millan, shrine of the old saint
who was also a comrade in arms of St James. There are two
monasteries here – Suso and Yuso – and I merely sat around
in these wondrous stone palaces trying to locate myself and
my relationship with God, something we often forget about
but which then becomes deeply and compellingly relevant
in such places.

I was on my own in the chapel and directly ahead of me
was an empty choir stall and a stone altar with a glimmering
bank of candles at its foot. The place was silent except for
an occasional creak of wood or a distant bell. A few words
came from somewhere but these were all the sounds of the
monastery itself: sounds without echoes, silent sounds, the
sounds of contemplative prayer.

You can excavate around your inner being for hours in
such places simply by sitting there watching those bars of
light stretching across that altar. Here you can also pick up
not only something of the tenderness of God but a sense of
his enduring strength too. Various bunches of wild flowers
stood on the altar. That distant bell again.

A monk came in and re-arranged the candles on the altar
before standing there and staring down at them prayerfully
for a while. Monks' lives often seem to be but long songs
of devotion but what goes on in a monk's mind? He disappeared in a series of softly diminishing footfalls and a fly
landed on the top of the pew in front of me before looking
around and taking off again.

The silence was complete and I tried to work out what
makes a monastic silence so different from any other
silence. Quite what was it about the quality of this silence
which binds each day into each week into each month and

into each year? This is the silence of centuries, the unity of unceasing prayer, in which a monk can develop a serious and full relationship with God away from the ruinous and noisy distractions of the city.

The treasures and paintings of the monastery, which are on display to the visitor, for a fee, seemed to me to be pretty ordinary, if not dusty, but it wasn't so much what the monastery contained that was so captivating as its position, way out here in the mountains and high up a valley. How did they get all that stone up here in the first place? The roads out here are pretty bad now and must have been absolutely awful back in the seventh century.

The valley was a church in itself and, after visiting both Yuso and Suso, I was reluctant to leave the area, pulling off the mountain road and into a forest when I spotted a clearing. The rays of the setting sun struck the roof of the forest. Every dip in the landscape was bathed in a golden light similar to that made by the candles on that stone altar. The stream hissed and gurgled like a congregation mumbling the Apostles' Creed and, with the early evening turning into darkness, the whole of the forest became one long fervent prayer.

I ate, read and slept well that night and was woken early in the morning by the rain drumming on the camper's roof like someone urgently banging to be let in. I decided I wouldn't leave this clearing until the weather had settled down again, noticing that this rain at least kept down the rampant insect life you often find in such wild places.

The sun soon began breaking through and rose over the red sandstone mountains, actually making the trees and high boulders boil with sheets of steam rising up out of them before splitting this way and that, like so many ghosts surging up out of a graveyard and off on a mass haunting somewhere, even if they weren't yet quite sure where.

As the sun reached the clearing, the morning started

filling up with bird song and the various small noises of the myriad insects who were all up and about again: the dancing butterflies, the zooming wasps and the luminous midges. I enjoyed sitting there and watching these changes of mood. Nothing ever seemed to quite stay the same for more than ten minutes, particularly in this weather and I almost felt I had been a part of a fine service of worship, out here alone in the duelling sun and rain.

But this was where the early Celts had always conducted their services: out in the fields and forests, among the insects and animals and as close as possible to God. Such places, in a sense, were the first monasteries of them all.

7

A Cathedral of Chickens

Your average Spanish village has a sweet fiesta simplicity about it but I never could quite suss out the larger towns in the North; graceless, sprawling places, for the most part, with a patina of economic dereliction. Obscure shops stood next to one another on the high street, with nothing obvious for sale, and any number of café bars, often empty of everything except a flickering television. You can sometimes sit in such places for up to two hours before anyone takes any notice of you.

Yet such superficial impressions of poverty were often undermined by the number of banks you also found in the high street. Even shops which looked like an estate agent's or a chemist's turned out, on closer inspection, to be another bank. In themselves these banks told a secret story of money and their sheer numbers suggested whole rivers of the stuff were flowing through subterranean passages in these parts, unwilling to show themselves to the world at large.

The people themselves seemed poor enough and everywhere there were those small booths selling lottery tickets – those weeds that always grow with such profusion in the famine-haunted gardens of poor people's dreams. *In fifteen days you will have to go back to work*, their posters said in English. *Or maybe not.*

Secret rivers of money generally flow in full flood almost everywhere in the world and you can also be sure they are always flowing from the deep pockets of the rich to the even deeper pockets of the even richer. This must be true of Spain where, on the evidence of your eyes in the high street, you can safely assume that money is always moving in great quantities and almost always for the benefit of the rich. Money is always piled high in the interstices of every society and, albeit secretly, almost always runs it. If you ever want to crack open a racket, any decent investigative reporter will tell you, follow the money.

Even if you want to understand the roots of a holy enterprise like pilgrimage you often only need to follow the money. Medieval pilgrimages were often first set up by monks in certain shrines to attract pilgrims who would bring their money. Local economies were built on pilgrim money and there is a sense in which the medieval pilgrimage was the first version of our modern package tourist industry.

Where, today, the advertising agencies promise dazzling dreams of sun, sand and sex, the equally creative medieval monks spun story after story around 'authentic' relics: of enough bits of the True Cross to make a new Spanish galleon, of bones of the saints, of statues which wept and visions that sang and danced . . . you name it and they dreamed it up, all in an effort to attract the pilgrim and his money.

It follows from this that those old monks probably got away with more fraud than the biggest swindlers in our modern financial markets, particularly when you consider there would have been almost no one – in the police, judiciary or the media – who would have had the clout to stand up against these monks and their fraudulent claims. Virtually anyone could take a plank of wood and say it came from the True Cross or come up with a dress which the Holy Mother used when she went shopping or put some water in a phial and claim that it was the sweat from Christ's brow as he hung on the cross. They could and did, all in the cause of attracting the pilgrim and parting him from his money. Those old monks made things true merely by saying they were true. It would have been a big, brave man who would have dared stand up and call them a liar. Luther tried it and look at the trouble the Vatican tried to heap on his head.

Christ was a trenchant and radical critic of money and he spoke of it more times than any other subject except the Kingdom of God. You cannot worship God and Mammon, he kept insisting. Woe to the rich. Blessed are the poor. Give until you bleed. He understood money was a dark and implacable power; demonic and destructive by nature. It had become a god in its own right which was worshipped by many. This god would seek control of our minds and hearts and then keep us enslaved because the urge to acquire money would never, ever be satisfied. We all know of the wealthy who spend every waking hour trying to become more wealthy, never so much as thinking of giving anything to the poor. When Jesus cleansed the temple in his only known act of violence he was saying, symbolically, how the land had to be first cleansed of Mammon. But today Mammon reigns more or less unmolested wherever you look and every political attempt to break this power has failed.

Such was the drift of my general thoughts while sitting in the square in Santo Domingo de la Calzada, my next stop on the *Camino*, a relentlessly ordinary Spanish town with the usual curious shops and multiplying banks and those ubiquitous storks watching over everything. A man was sitting next to me with his eyes closed as he lifted his face happily to the sun. Two pilgrims were sitting in the shade of a tree licking ice creams.

The cathedral here is a singular place since, in the nave

and just above the door leading down to the crypt, there is a cage containing chickens which is one of the must-see pilgrim features in Spain.

The story goes that a young Frenchman and his family were passing this way in the fifteenth century when the boy took the fancy of a local Spanish girl in an inn here. But he refused to have anything to do with her and, mightily miffed, she hid some silver in his belongings and, when he had gone on his way, reported the 'theft' to the police. He was immediately hauled back here, tried and hanged. When his heartbroken parents returned this way a few weeks later they passed the gallows and their son, who was evidently still hanging there, said: 'I am not dead. Saint James saved me. I am alive.'

The parents went to the local justice who was in the middle of eating roast chicken. 'If he is alive, then the cock and hen here on my plate are going to start crowing,' the judge snorted whereupon the cock crowed and the hen cackled. The judge ordered the young man to be cut down and everyone lived happily ever after.

I visited the cathedral where I wandered in a small pilgrim museum which had the usual collection of treasures and an abundance of ornate processional crosses. I was fascinated by the tiny skull of a medieval pilgrim, complete with his original hat and old sandals. There was also the skeleton of a small mouse which may well have been the same pilgrim's pet mouse.

The Visitors' Book revealed that a few English pilgrims had been this way recently: 'Bello! Bello! Bello!' wrote Greta and Brian Cooper; 'May we all be in Christ as he prayed,' wrote Canon John Bowers of St Boniface Church, Cheshire; Derek and Stephanie Smith added they liked being able to wander around on their own and turn on the lights.

Inside the nave the cock and hen were puffing up their chests and flapping their wings as they jumped around inside their ecclesiastical prison above a crumbling crypt door. They are changed twice a month but I felt sorry for them, stuck up there with nothing much to look at except the backs of the Sunday morning congregations and gawping pilgrims like me. Part of the original Frenchman's gallows is embedded in a wall directly opposite the chicken cage. Or so they say.

Now half a minute's quiet reflection on this whole sorry business of those two chickens coming alive underneath the judge's poised knife and fork can only lead to the conclusion that the story is the purest nonsense. Everything about the story is suspect, not least the way the young lad hung on the gallows for a fortnight, thought to be dead and coming alive just as his parents happened to be strolling past. Not even Paul Daniels can do that.

But a further half a minute's reflection will also tell you this story is quite a good story as it goes – it's not *Gone With The Wind*, it's true, but it's all right – and so, somewhere in the past, we can safely assume that some bright spark, somewhere here in Santo Domingo de la Calzada, doubtless seeking to improve the peseta flow into the cathedral, had thought well, we've got the story, which, *entre nous*, is certainly rubbish, but what we'll do now is get some chickens in here to beef up the story a bit, in a manner of speaking, and, before Ash Wednesday had got to Christmas Eve, they'd put in a chicken cage above the crypt door, installed a few live chickens and, lo, it did indeed work – and how! – since these chickens must now be the most-photographed chickens in the whole of Christendom as armies of pilgrims make their way here with their Instamatics since pilgrims, just like everyone else, are always suckers for a good story and a fuzzy snap.

No pilgrim now goes through Santo Domingo de la Calzada without visiting these chickens and pilgrims mean – and have always meant – money.

The Road next opened out onto the plains of Castile and I was constantly stopping to admire the wild flowers which were growing in such profusion along its banks. There were red poppies, light blue cornflowers, yellow buttercups and white dog daisies – lovely, multicoloured necklaces of wildness in which grasshoppers jumped, butterflies fluttered, small lizards slithered and bees zoomed from flower to flower doing whatever bees do.

We were amongst huge rolling fields of wheat but the weather had turned cold again, blowing hostile winds into the faces of the pilgrims who had to bend low to struggle against them. Dust was another discomfort as were the odd showers of freezing rain which kept breaking through the uncertain sunshine. The distant mountains were actually capped with snow. *Snow*! I couldn't believe it, They didn't even have snow on the summit of Snowdon, the highest mountain in Wales, in the middle of summer, and here we were allegedly in the middle of sunny Spain.

A couple of inches of snow had fallen on Madrid that week, according to a news report on the radio. So, if it wasn't Swiss Alps snow it was Wimbledon fortnight rain, and I was again composing a letter of complaint to the Advertising Standards Authority in London about that campaign by the Spanish Tourist Board which was forever banging on about sunny Spain. Any legal action against them over this might well be the easiest ever prosecution under the Trades Description Act.

That wild and windy morning, however, was considerably enlivened when I spotted a ruined monastery just off the road and I pulled in to have a nose around it. The garden walls were made of mud and straw but had long fallen down in many places. The old vegetable beds were overgrown and the windows in the main house broken. Evidently many pilgrims had spotted this place before me since there was a sign specifically warning *peregrinos* to keep out. They hadn't and I discovered a ruined chapel with an old sleeping bag strewn across the floor and an Iron Maiden T-shirt carefully draped over the altar. A dozen or so empty beer bottles lay around in disarray and one of the walls had been badly scorched by a fire.

The absence of prayer is always marked in formerly holy places like this. It has been scoured out of the building by the rogue winds and the smell of stale beer. I moved slowly down the corridor upstairs, opening one door after another and looking into each room. They were empty of everything except the odd, stained mattress and lots of flies but, even so, I soon found myself knocking softly on the doors before I went in, perhaps worried I might come across some old monk who had been left behind in the exodus; some ancient sentinel who would look up from his prayer book and say: 'Yes, my son. Can I be of any help to you?'

I was tense with the expectancy of coming across something or someone but it was merely a story of lots of birds rushing about in the rafters and the occasional fat spider whizzing the length of his cobweb to get out of my way. One room towards the end of the corridor was full of unexpected sunlight, the walls and floorboards so intensely brilliant I couldn't see any cracks or dust, just this bright gold veneer that practically begged me to stand in the middle of it and feel like some Greek god basking in the warmth of daybreak on the slopes of Mount Olympus. This sunlight even had a soothing music in it; a new music somewhat at odds with the dereliction of this ruined monastery. But the sunshine disappeared abruptly and the cold squeezed my calves as yet another light shower of rain

fell through the huge holes in the roof, bringing back all
the damp, dull emblems of ruin and decay.

I stood at the broken window watching the rain coming
down into the courtyard and trying to picture what it must
have been like here: horses drinking in that fountain, perhaps, as the monks went about their days of work and
prayer with the hours marked off by the bells. And why
then had they abandoned it? What brought them here in the
first place and, more to the point, what had then driven
them away? Fear? Despair? Starvation?

Outside, at the bottom of the wild garden, I found a
genuine oddity – a huge standing cross, about thirty feet
high and ten feet across, made entirely of welded oil drums.
Now why would anyone have put such an ugly thing here?
And who had made it? Clearly not the monks of old. You
could probably construct quite an interesting novel simply
around what I had discovered here in the last hour.

That night, in a camp site just before Burgos, I met an
engaging pair of men whom I came to know as the Mayor
and the Architect, who were walking to Compostela even if
it wasn't quite in the traditional manner. Ruud was the
Mayor and Franz was the Architect and they had been
walking The Road since 11 April. They averaged 30 kilo-
metres a day, they said and knew exactly at what time and
on what day they were going to arrive in Compostela. Their
wives had even booked the plane tickets to be there to greet
them.

But these were no ordinary pilgrims since they had a
driver with a caravan who set up a base camp somewhere
along the route every five days or so. This driver prepared
their meals, picked them up each afternoon, and, after a
good night's sleep in the caravan, ferried them back to
wherever they had last left off their walk. My (unaired)

suspicions about the validity and propriety of such a pilgrimage were considerably thickened when they also said they carried a mobile phone to call up their driver if they ever got into difficulty or wanted something quickly like an umbrella to cope with the rain.

Ruud, a tall, Steve McQueen look-a-like with fierce blue eyes and lots of gold teeth, explained to me that being a mayor in Holland was actually a proper profession. He is appointed by the Queen and has a pension and various fringe benefits like a car with a chauffeur and presumably all the tulip bulbs he can carry home. There were 15,000 people in his village and his job was to see that everything worked properly.

Franz, the Architect, a swarthy man bursting with good health, had once worked for the Mayor and they had discovered they had a lot in common. Eventually they decided to do this walk for all kinds of reasons. The Mayor thought the walk would help him to look back on his past which would then set him up for his future. The Architect said he had deep religious reasons for doing the walk and hoped it would bring him closer to God.

They had both been amazed at the appalling houses they had seen in Spain – 'dirty and squalid like caves' – although they both liked the country, especially the people, the scenery and the bird-life. They spoke about everything under the sun when they walked together, they said and I sensed – although they never actually told me so – they were almost certainly forging a friendship which was going to last the rest of their lives.

Cities are often like people in that you either take to them immediately or you don't ever. I took to Burgos, the capital of Castile, almost immediately and I wasn't sure why particularly as the weather continued to be unpredictable, to put it mildly. They even have a little joke about the weather in Burgos which was that the summer begins here on the day of St James, 26 July, only to come to an end again on the day of St Ann, the very next day.

Almost the first thing you see in Burgos is the magnificent city gate, which is more like a castle which has somehow lost her interior, although any pomp that might be attendant on this gate was immediately deflated by a large sign for McDonald's hamburgers right next to it. *Mon dieu*, you wouldn't catch the French allowing anything as vulgar as that.

Then, as you move down through the thrumming streets, making in the direction of the cathedral, as all good pilgrims do, you pick up on a certain relaxed orderliness, with many people going about their business, large plazas full of formal flower beds and benches where you can sit in the drizzle and dream extravagant dreams of sun hitting the golden sands of Mediterranean beaches. And there are all those old, dark buildings which look as though they are about to fall apart. This city was also a well-known centre for the church and military, as you can still see by the numbers of nuns and men in uniforms mingling on the pavements. The military even had their own park.

Everything had a lovely flair about it and all this city seemed to lack was somewhere to park, a problem which was considerably worsened by the way people seemed not to park their cars on the sides of the roads so much as abandon them in the middle, causing traffic jams everywhere.

I braked in one plaza, out of the main line of the traffic, and sat there, trying to work out what to do next, when a man came up to me and knocked on my window which I wound down half-expecting to be handed a parking ticket. But, far from being a traffic warden, it turned out he was a puppeteer with quite good English and a glass eye which was a forget-me-not blue in startling contrast to his good one which was a dull brown. He was planning to work the streets of London this autumn, he said, so did I think he would make much money doing that?

This is not a question I get asked too often so I hummed and hawed, saying that I didn't think Londoners were meaner than anywhere else so, yes, he would probably do all right. What sort of clothes should he take with him to London? More humming and hawing, punctuated by a fair bit of blowing. Well, the warm clothes you might wear here at that time of year, I suppose. What if he fell sick? Well, if he fell really sick he might well die, I thought but I kept my thoughts to myself, adding that London hospitals were rated as highly as anywhere else in the world. And what if . . .

I had to go, I said. I shouldn't be parked here and had better find somewhere to stop legally or the law would grab me. He understood, he said with a rather strange wink of his good eye and a rather wild stare from his forget-me-not blue one, waving me goodbye and saying we would probably meet again in London.

I did find somewhere to park on some strangely empty blue lines and further explored the old city before coming across one of those marvellous cafés where they set out the menu in small pictures. So I ordered a picture of a plate of bacon, egg and sausage, together with a picture of a cup of coffee, which I was enjoying when I was aware of a lot of activity under my tablecloth and around the whereabouts of my feet. It turned out to be a gypsy who, without so much as a word or by-your-leave, was now busily polishing my shoes only to occasionally look up and shout 'Oi' as he cracked his brushes together flamboyantly. It seemed a bit late to stop him – which was clearly part of the sales plan – and, after a bit of a quarrel over the fee, he went off clutching what must certainly have been far too many pesetas for the job.

I guess he must have then told one of his gypsy pals that there was some British fool eating bacon and egg in the café over the road since I was just finishing my meal when there was a flash of a gold ear-ring and I spotted another one diving for my feet and I lifted them both up into the air shouting 'No, no, no,' so loudly the restaurant proprietor came out and ushered him away.

A whole gang of them was working the streets of Burgos with the children begging, the men playing instruments or polishing the shoes of the unwary and the women selling sprigs of lucky pine. Their antics as they hustled the passers-by made me smile even if I did keep nervously fingering my wallet to see that it was still there.

I recalled the way they had hustled whole gangs of pilgrims in Rome. The children, in particular, would carry large strips of cardboard to conceal the movements of their hands while they relieved pilgrims of their wallets or cameras and there is no sight quite so funny as a small child holding a strip of cardboard wandering down a Roman pavement and a whole gang of pilgrims spotting this child and literally turning on their heels and running away as fast as they could go.

There is nothing hangdog about gypsies either; nothing, for example, of that air of defeat and desolation that pervades those who sit in the waiting rooms of doctors and dentists. Gypsies are always up for it in the current jargon; always seem to have a smile on their lips and a pocketful of money and, on the one and only time I have ever been arrested for being drunk and disorderly – in the Balls Pond Road in London after an argument with a policeman who was stopping black motorists – I ended up in a cell in Holloway with a whole mob of them who, hungover and contrite, paid their fines the next morning taking out rolls of money the size of small cabbages from concealed pockets with one even offering to pay my £6 fine, if I was 'a bit short'.

Burgos cathedral is said to be the finest Gothic cathedral in Spain and yet her great glory, it seemed to me as I wandered around inside her, was she seemed to have the fingerprints of almost every other great cathedral I have ever wandered around inside. Wherever I looked and from whatever angle, I found myself thinking of other cathedrals.

The treasures in the museum seemed every bit as extravagant and opulent as those in St Peter's in Rome; the huge high tower holding that great explosion of sunshine reminded me of the much smaller Lantern Tower in Ely Cathedral; the ravishing altar and ornate wooden choir stalls had echoes of Chartres and there was the octagonal window, glittering with stellar bursts of coloured light, as in Notre Dame or York.

The place added up to a non-stop display of Gothic and Renaissance art and there was something beautiful or impressive wherever you turned from the great central nave to the elaborate choir and that marbled stairway going nowhere. Everything was worked with such delicacy, drama and care they chimed together deep in you as you considered the sheer scale of these incredibly artistic responses to the majesty of God. An age of unbelief and materialism simply could not produce a building with such riches. A cathedral like this could only have been put together by workmen who had a relationship with God running at the very deepest levels of their being. Such art, riches and workmanship could only have been produced by real believers drawing on every ounce of their artistic resources and reaching deep into their hearts solely that they might give honour to God.

Even from high on the pine-scented hill outside you could also see the centrality of the cathedral to the life of Burgos by the way it sat at the centre of everything in a low spin of hills with all the modern buildings and parks radiating out from it until they disappeared into the wheat fastnesses of Castile.

This cathedral also contains the tomb of El Cid and his wife Ximena. El Cid, whose real name was Rodrigo Diez de Vivar, was a strange and shadowy warrior of ice and flame whose victories over the Moors made him famous; *The Song of El Cid* turned him into a national hero. He stormed all over these parts nine centuries ago, a mercenary at first who did his best to destroy the Moors and Christians with a complete impartiality. He ravaged Rioja and levelled Logroño, also later capturing the Kingdom of Valencia. This campaign was initially fought on behalf of King Alfonso of León and Castile but later became a private venture, begun in 1088 and continuing until his capture of the town in 1094. His oddest triumph came when he was dead and his corpse was strapped to his horse, so putting the wind up the Moors that he caused a complete rout.

So he takes his place with St James as one of the national heroes of the *Reconquista* and news of his death swept along The Road down to Compostela and out into Europe. 'Away in Spain, in Valencia, Don Rodrigo has died, to the grief of Christendom and the joy of the pagan,' wrote a French monk in 1099, the year of his death.

Many of El Cid's bloody exploits took place in Burgos which is dotted with statues and other memorials commemorating a life of all-out rampage. One had a few severed Moorish heads scattered at the feet of his horse. But his moment of real fame came when Hollywood took a look at his life and he was portrayed by Charlton Heston. Yet the real El Cid can have been nothing at all like Charlton Heston as I discovered for myself once when I interviewed

Heston when he had come to London promoting his auto-biography. Unlike El Cid, red in tooth and claw, ready to knock over whole cities if they looked at him the wrong way, Charlton Heston was, I thought, neither very inter-esting nor very dull and certainly not remotely capable of hurting anyone or anything, no matter how they might have looked at him. He seemed to have no particularly rampant bees in his bonnet; he had made up his mind about everything and it was a bit like talking to an extremely polite policeman who, you knew, was simply listening to your side of things and was going to book you, no matter what you said.

His eyes were not so much bright blue as the soft, neutral colour of stone and his short orange hair looked suspiciously like a hairpiece. There were the finely honed cheekbones and the smile like an empty poster hoarding. He com-plained a lot about the way his career had been hampered by his biblical and Renaissance image – of how it was dif-ficult to get anyone to take you seriously when they kept calling you Moses or El Cid or asking you where you had tied up the chariot – and how he was hoping his autobio-graphy was going to set the record straight and stop all the cheap jibes.

Unfortunately his autobiography was dire and the best that could be said about it was that it was so big that, if you dropped it, it would break your toe.

8

Misery on the Meseta

The toughest part of the pilgrimage for the walker comes after Burgos – trudging across the parched hills and fertile lowlands of the *meseta* with sections so high and dry they were almost desert and others so low and wet the land was heaving with growth in this, one of the main bread-baskets of Spain.

Pilgrims are always warned to set out early in these parts to avoid the heat of the midday sun but again it wasn't too hot that morning with fat, black clouds roaming the skies ominously as the pilgrims set out in singles and groups across those huge plains surrounded by even huger horizons. The scene was almost biblical as they seemed to be trooping into the very dawn of time with their staves and floppy pilgrim hats as the odd pillars of sunlight propped up the edges of those roaming black clouds. These plains were famous for their mirages and shadows of things which were not there. Swarms of locusts had once descended on these plains and eaten everything in sight. Plague germs had worked their deadly way through local villages.

Pilgrims had even been known to die in some numbers on the *meseta* and, in a plaza in the down-at-heel and fly-blown fortress town of nearby Castrojeriz, they had found, under the paving stones, the skeleton of a medieval pilgrim surrounded by scallop shells and fourteenth-century coins.

I passed ruined *adobe* houses, dried-up water fountains and the remnants of old sheep pens. Yet more fields were amok with smoke and flames as the farm workers burned off the stubble. More old and ruined houses were scattered around old and ruined churches in Fromista where the storks were still standing around in their ragged eyries as pilgrims sat in the shelter of church doorways taking a rest or having their lunch. You must eat small amounts and often while walking The Road. Just keep shovelling it down as you go along. Here I also came across a statue of a man who was associated with St Elmo's fire, a discharge of natural electricity down a ship's mast.

Carrion de los Condes came and went and I spent some time wandering on my own in the *meseta* again, enjoying the odd hour of sunlight as it played around in the waving heads of the wheat. It was so vast but it was also pretty much impossible to get lost out here, I discovered, since, whenever you were unsure of your direction, all you had to do was stop still, look around and wait. Sooner or later you would be bound to spot, moving through the shimmering wheat, yet another group of pilgrims, making their way to Compostela with all the dedicated urgency that keeps a salmon fighting up river or a herd of wildebeest crossing the Savannah.

This was a good section of the journey for me since I could feel my spirit soaking up this strange and riven landscape. I was also eating and sleeping well with no alcohol. Lourdes had continued to do a good job on me because I remained pretty much unworried about my health even if I still got tired and leaden by about six o'clock. Yet I *was* surprised at how much I was missing my wife.

I took two Yugoslavian students to the outskirts of León before dropping them off at a supermarket and plunging into the city on my own, hoping to catch the famed cathedral before it closed. I'm still not sure what happened but the long and short of it was I found the city's traffic system impenetrable. This was Spaghetti Junction Spanish-style since three times I tried to head for the cathedral and three times I ended up somewhere I didn't want to be only to return three times, to the place I had started from. The whole drive was positively Kafkaesque and I had a startling new insight into the causes of road rage as I again ended up outside the San Marcos Hotel and nowhere near the cathedral I wanted to visit.

Right, a good night's sleep was called for so I headed back out of the city the way I had come in, finding a rather crowded camp site near a church and next to a stream where it looked as if quite a few other pilgrims, possibly as defeated as me, had decided to bed down for the night before taking on León, fresh and first thing in the morning.

I am not exactly sure why I always found the sight of these pilgrims quite so inspiring, some of them washing their clothes or themselves in the stream, others cooking up meals on their little primuses and a few sitting around a young man strumming a guitar. This might well have been medieval times, a ragged army in a tented city laying siege to the ramparts of this cathedral city of León which they were going to capture with the help of the ferocious power of their prayer and the integrity of their pilgrimage.

Most of the pilgrims on The Road were Spanish. Lots of Spanish youth groups seemed to turn up everywhere and two Spanish priests had done the pilgrimage together every year for the last fifteen years. One Spanish family, I heard, were taking it in turns to lead their blind father to Compostela and he had found that walking The Road was the best way to get to know your children.

The Spanish were closely followed by the French and Dutch in almost equal measure. Then the Germans, the Americans and a sprinkling of Brits. I hadn't yet met a British pilgrim although I had heard of plenty of them including a 75-year-old member of the House of Lords who was a shy sort, according to the gossip, but quite chatty when he got going, claiming that he had a mother who was more than 100 years old. Some do it on their vacations for a week or a fortnight each year, coming back the next year and taking it up wherever they had left it off.

Another group of German Catholics were doing the pilgrimage in a minibus and, having worked out their route, half of them set off first thing in the morning to arrange food and a camp site. The other half walked it and the next day they set off to find food and a camp site. This meant that they walked half the distance with plenty of rest which was one way of doing it, I guess.

I spent a few happy hours with Dan Ruunde, a 25-year-old from New York, who spoke knowledgeably about the country, particularly the way the ghost of General Franco still seemed to haunt the Spanish and how many – particularly the elderly – would like to have the old scoundrel back to re-establish law 'n' order which many perceive as having gone to the dogs.

Dan had been staying in a lot of *refugios* but was getting fed up with them, smelly as they often were with the pilgrims' 'blood, sweat and tears'. Most showered every night, it seemed, but a lot didn't. They also snored like it was going out of fashion at any minute. He often got out of bed in the middle of the night to open a window for some fresh air but it was almost always a Spaniard who closed it again.

'The Spanish also use the *refugios* as a cheap way of bed and breakfast, parking their cars around the corner and carrying in their bags, claiming they are genuine pilgrims,' Dan added darkly. 'I'm doing this for adventure but my motive is mainly spiritual. You always pay for your sins and, out here on the *Camino*, you pay for your sins in full. This pilgrimage sort of makes you feel good about yourself – even when you're feeling pretty bad, if you get my drift.'

When I woke the next morning the whole of the medieval tented army had packed up and gone off to lay siege to León without me. Not a single one of them was left and neither had they left any litter, merely disappeared into the morning air like so much mist and leaving me to commune with a cup of tea and write up a few notes on the bank of the stream.

But I had got used to the inherent loneliness of The Road by now and had anyway never enjoyed travelling in groups. You can't dive off the route following a whim when you are in a group and I usually ended up quarrelling with someone, often the group leader, when I was in a group. I was even thrown out of the cubs for being a disruptive influence so it is far better for everyone, I have long learned, for me to stay on my own when I will only end up getting on my own nerves.

I sat down with a road map and guide book to get me to the cathedral in León but, even after the most careful preparation, found myself going one way and another before ending up outside the San Marcos Hotel again, said to be one of the best hotels in the world, so I went inside to have a look around that.

I'm not very keen on posh hotels – or the sort of people who patronize them – but such hotels or *paradors* are, in a way, central to the pilgrim story here since they are often historic buildings or monasteries or old pilgrim hostels which have been taken over – grabbed? – by the government and turned into luxury hotels. This one in León was a pilgrim hospice as far back as the twelfth century when it was overseen by the mighty Order of Santiago. It was later developed several times incorporating a new monastery and a church, in a rich Gothic style, and is one of the city's principal tourist attractions. The huge facade, profusely carved and decorated with busts of many famous figures, as well as a rampant St James wielding a sword on horseback, is so self-important it might even serve as the home for a vital centre of government.

Yet there is, perhaps predictably, nothing genuinely pilgrim about the cost of the rooms, at around £100 a night, and they are not terribly interested in the ragged or the down-at-heel here. But you can always wander around inside the place, if you do so with a certain confidence and panache, striding down the corridors purposively as if you own the joint. It was a most impressive collection of stone stairways and chandeliered rooms, many furnished with expensive antiques. Outside in the cloisters there were lots of high stone statues with pigeons burbling in the morning sunshine. Lots of the carved faces on the cloister walls had lost their noses but, back inside, everything hummed with a polished efficiency. Every feature – from the odd writing tables to the tapestries on the walls – must have cost an arm and a leg while the bar itself was piled high with so much expensive daftness it might have been a collision between a Bedouin tent and a Harry Ramsden's fish and chip restaurant. You simply couldn't sit in all this fussy tat and have a quiet drink without laughing your head off.

But it was a shame, in some ways, that such studied extravagance was only available to the seriously rich and certainly not the likes of most everyone I had so far met on The Road. Not that I regretted being unable to stay here myself since, even when I was on an unlimited newspaper expense account, I would never pay out £100 simply to put my head down for the night – no matter how sumptuous the surroundings which are always exactly the same in the dark and when you are asleep. You can also still get bad dreams no matter how much you pay for a bed.

I found León cathedral, in the end, by the revolutionary method of walking there on my own two feet, marvelling at the boulevards and fountains of this medieval city which has long been bound up with the pilgrim cult of Santiago.

The old quarter positively revels in the charm of the
Middle Ages although I immediately missed my beloved
camper when one of the chintzy cafés stung me for a little
more than £2 for a fizzy orange drink. These prices always
get me down – they are at it almost everywhere a pilgrim
goes – although, if you are thirsty, there is nothing you
can do about it. I have died too many deaths in too many
distant flyblown lavatories to ever drink the water from a
public fountain and nothing would persuade me to eat an
ice cream almost anywhere in Europe – or an oyster for that
matter.

The cathedral touched something deep in your pilgrim
heart as you rubbed your palm over the smooth stone
column at the entrance, just as so many other pilgrims have
done before. It was begun in 1205 and is a prime example
of a pure Gothic art. The nave is as high as it is wide but
its chief glory is the 182 stained glass windows which cover
all the three major rose windows and most of the cathedral's
walls to the extent that, as you look up around you, it feels
as if you are riding the cockpit of a spaceship constructed
solely out of pure light as it makes its long and fabulous
journey to Mars.

Shafts of light kept moving around me as I turned and
turned again with my eyes picking out saints, plants and
angels going about their work in the windows. A central
depiction of the Madonna in the rose window in the north
transept radiated celestial shafts of light.

Elsewhere in the cathedral there were scenes of the
Nativity, choir stalls sculpted out of black walnut and a
chapel dedicated to St James, built in the sixteenth century
and with yet more ravishing stained glass and yet more
angels flying around the walls. St James himself was seated
in the middle of it all near the Virgin del Camino (who she?)
who was holding the body of a large, dead Christ.

The whole cathedral must have been a terrific inspiration

to the flagging pilgrim as he then set out again, to make his way west, into the eye of the setting sun and onwards to the real shrine of St James in Compostela.

It was no accident, I suppose, that I finally managed to locate León cathedral on my own two feet since that's how you are supposed to travel on The Road. But the nearer I got to Compostela the more I realized that pilgrims were up to all sorts of tricks to make their pilgrimage easier.

Colm Toibin, in his travel book, *The Sign of the Cross*, gives a hilarious account of how he set out to walk from León to Compostela but almost immediately got fed up in the cold drizzle and caught a train to Astorga. From here he walked in the wrong direction for a while before realizing his mistake and taking a taxi back to Astorga where he caught the bus to Ponferrada and from there to Villafranca. On this bus they were showing, appropriately enough, *The Silence of the Lambs* and he kept being woken up by other passengers' screams. Then he hitch-hiked in what he admitted was 'public, bare-faced cheating' before getting off in Galicia. He did walk for a day or two but it was back to a taxi and bus before taking a train for the rest of the journey to Santiago. He was, to be fair to him, riven by good old Catholic guilt about the whole business.

I never met anyone who did it quite as haphazardly as this but I was told in León about a Dutch woman who had a two-stroke engine attached to the back wheel of her bicycle 'for the hills and mountains'. Then there was the Mayor and the Architect and I could never quite make up my mind about that. I was also worried about the German Catholics who were doing half of it although here in León I heard another story about the Belgian man who was doing the whole journey by taxi. Yet he seemed to have had something of an excuse since he had twisted his ankle soon after he had started out with his mates from Roncesvalles. He didn't want to return home so, while his mates walked, he went by taxi ahead of them, booked the hotel and welcomed them when they stumbled in. Every night he rang his wife back home to tell her he was getting on fine and they were well on course. The second rule of pilgrimage: Don't worry your partner back home.

And that night, in a field outside Astorga, just before the high, ragged mountains of León, I was surrounded by a pilgrim gang doing it yet another way. I had eaten and was enjoying the sunset when I heard a lot of throaty roaring of motor bikes coming from a distant wood. They swooped down towards me and pulled up around my camper like a motorized tribe of Red Indians before spending the next hour tuning and oiling their wretched engines until, unable to stand it any longer, I drove to the furthest corner of the field and scrabbled around under the back seat until I found the tin marked ear-plugs.

Astorga was another lively medieval town and the next pilgrim staging post on the *Camino* where, in the heyday of the pilgrimage, they had no less than 24 pilgrim hostels. Not much was going on when I fetched up there, parking next to the cathedral on some blue lines and visiting the Bishop's Palace, a strange and fantastically ornate place designed by the famous Catalan architect, Antonio Gaudi who also dreamed up the Sagrada Familia in Barcelona.

This place was quite modest when set beside the eccentric and thrilling creation that is the Sagrada Familia but you soon picked up on his strange brush-strokes as you walked into this Palace. You kept thinking your eyes were deceiving you as you looked hard and noticed that not one single line was straight. The patterns, on closer inspection, turned out not to be patterns. Shapes started like the usual shapes but then got tortured. Huge internal doorways without doors opened up onto yet more huge doorways without doors. There was no privacy here. The Bishop couldn't even mutter a few heretical words about the Pope without having it overheard three floors down. And it was freezing cold with the young girl attendants wearing thick socks – even in the middle of summer. One was fast asleep.

Rooms were rich with Moorish ceramics and the Bishop's throne room was arrogant beyond belief. I entered a room full of medieval paintings in which the ubiquitous St James was portrayed with Christ. St James was wearing his usual woollen hat with a scallop-shell fixed with hat-pins. A huge map also showed the many pick 'n' mix pilgrim routes to Compostela; so many, in fact, you were by now virtually convinced the authorities must have made them up as they went along: 'Now this part of Galicia is not doing too well so next week we'll run a new pilgrim path through there.'

The whole Palace was Gaudi at his maddest and the only question that ever occurs to me when I look around at the strange and exuberant emblems of his mind is, how did he ever get permission to put up buildings like this in the first place? Everything about his work was so out of whack with everything else it was a wonder that he wasn't just locked up or beheaded when he first suggested it. And how, more to the point, in this money-mad age, was he given millions of pesetas to get on with it? George Orwell said of his Sagrada Familia in Barcelona: 'One of the most hideous buildings in the world. The Anarchists showed bad taste when they didn't blow it up when they had a chance.'

There is no way of describing the Sagrada Familia. It's like nothing else that you have ever seen with no sense or form as you gaze up at those soaring towers which have been likened to all kinds of things from perforated cigars to celestial snooker cues. The towers are not straight and are tipped by eccentric ceramic pinnacles. The exterior stone walls simply drip like so many encrusted stalactites. Once inside the building your headache thickens and you don't have a clue what's going on. What starts where? Why is that there and not here?

If there was one man in history who I would have liked to have sat down with and had a good chat about what was on his mind it was Antonio Gaudi but, unfortunately, he was knocked down by a Barcelona tram in 1926 and there was a drawing of him lying on his death-bed here in the Bishop's Palace in Astorga, silent forever.

When I returned to my camper I found, tucked under my windscreen wiper, yet another small envelope with a lot of Spanish writing on it. I had collected quite a few of these on my travels through Spain but couldn't make any sense of them, assuming that they were inviting contributions to some charity like a sort of Spanish Oxfam or Christian Aid.

Yet, as I was looking at this envelope again, I heard a couple walking past speaking in English. Excuse me, but did they speak Spanish? They did and so I asked them what this envelope was all about. Ah, the woman said, after turning it one way and another. Far from inviting a contribution to Oxfam these envelopes were inviting me to put a parking fine into this envelope and post it right over there.

But I had parked on these blue lines many times. Ah yes, you can indeed park on these blue lines but you must pay for a parking ticket first and, if you don't, you get one of these envelopes asking you to pay a fine which you put in that letter box there. One day I was going to get the hang of Spain, but it clearly wasn't going to be for a long time yet. But what could you expect from a country which not only produced but then went on to revere one Antonio Gaudi?

9

Home of Celtic Mysticism

The *meseta* ended soon after Astorga and a vague but certain wildness inhabited the air as I threaded my way across a hilly landscape towards the mountains. Fir plantations mixed haphazardly with vineyards. Odd pilgrim stone crosses lined The Road and drystone walls marked out uneven plots.

A huge slagheap stood guard over the coal-mining town of Ponferrada and I found a ruined pilgrim hospice in the old quarter now giving hospitality only to pigeons. Everything was absolutely creaking with great age with wooden balconies just about managing to cling to the fronts of ramshackle houses which had green, moss-encrusted roofs and vines holding together their crumbling walls.

Then came Villafranca, the last stop before the dizzying climb into Galicia where the pilgrim track, marked only by the odd yellow daub, cut along the valley floors and up over peaks as it meandered towards the windy summits. You could lie at the bottom of those deep, empty valleys all year long, crying out in the most abject and pitiless agony, but only the eagles would hear you and they wouldn't much care anyway as they glided around and around their cold, wet kingdom of Galician mysteries.

But even in such a lonely place the rhythms of the pilgrimage were becoming more intense and I kept spotting tents in odd forest clearings or pilgrims washing their clothes or paddling in the cold streams. One minute there would be nothing except the moving mists and then a group of a dozen or so of them would come bursting out of this swirling, ghostly whiteness. A mangled and dead fox lay on the road, yet another flattened by passing traffic.

I had never for one minute realized this pilgrimage was so real and again I found my veins thickening with excitement as I watched them picking their way along boulder-strewn paths, lined by nettles and slithery with cow pats, shouldering the enormous weight of their back-packs and fluttering in their coloured rain capes, scratching their heads as they studied their maps or put yet more plasters on yet more blistered and torn feet or merely sat there on a grey rock, with mountain mists swirling all around them, enjoying a quiet fag.

These were very much my kind of people, gods all of them, unable to step forward and guzzle the national swill or lose themselves in the normal ways – in drink or drugs or television. They had left all that rubbish behind them as they struggled down The Road, accompanied only by their own moral seriousness and sense of quest, even if a lot of them didn't quite understand what that quest was. Oh aye, that age-old search for the spirit of God was alive and well for sure.

Later that day I passed a pack of wild dogs wandering down the side of the road and then another pack who, it must be said, didn't seem aggressive in the slightest, even if I wasn't exactly going to stand in front of them to find out for myself. The grass was thick and lush with purple patches of clover telling that same story of lots of rain. Heather mingled with gorse and broom. Chestnut trees surrounded pine forests. You could often pick up the taste of eucalyptus and I spotted a man wearing wooden shoes. Wild horses roamed the distant slopes and, down in the market, there was a lot of shellfish for sale with one man boiling up squid in a bucket, the small tentacles flailing around in the pink bubbles like some sort of witch's cocktail.

I had never been this way before but everything about this countryside seemed familiar. The sheer wildness of the place was stirring something within some deep ancestral/tribal/race memory of mine; a sensation impossibly vague and difficult to describe because that's exactly how it was. I couldn't quite put anything together when I finally got to the refuge at Cebrero, a group of sanctuary buildings high on the top of a mountain, set around a small church, a museum and a huge stone building complete with a high, conical thatched roof. It was while looking at this roof that the penny dropped.

I was clearly back in the lands of the Celts. These were the sort of homes favoured by the early Celts and even this tiny hamlet, with its marauding chickens and stone church, was like most any Welsh village stuck in the middle of some damp nowhere and with no visible means of support.

Galicia has long been known as the home of Celtic mysticism and perhaps what I had been sniffing in the air were the sights and smells of my own Welsh homeland – the damp, cold chapels, the cockerels strutting free along the ash paths, the packs of dogs wandering abroad, the wild horses, the sporadic stuttering of cold rain on a lonely, insecure people who had grown up beneath empty slate skies where they worshipped in the open air because that brought them close to the mind and heart of God.

Even road signs had been crossed out and replaced with what I took to be Gallego – just as our own Welsh nationalists like to do when they find themselves with a pot of paint, some energy and a free hour.

In keeping with her Celtic roots there are numerous legends in Galicia and here in Cebrero, founded in 836 to help the pilgrims get over these treacherous mountains, we come across the most enduring Celtic legend of them all – the Holy Grail.

Each morning a shepherd from a nearby hamlet used to come to Cebrero for communion, according to the legend, and, what is more, he always turned up come wind, snow or avalanche of which, you can be very sure, there was always a goodly number. The officiating priest, who would have preferred to have stayed tucked up in his warm bed, told this holy shepherd he must be as daft as a daffodil to travel all this way, in this awful weather, merely to worship simple bread and wine.

The heavens themselves turned over at this heretical remark since the bread immediately turned into human flesh and the wine in the chalice into blood. This trans-figuration, in its turn, took flight on many pilgrim tongues and soon became incorporated into the legend of the Holy Grail and the full name of this sanctuary became El Cebrero do Canto Grail.

The divine elements have been carefully preserved to this day, they say, and the reliquaries are still on display in the chapel where they sit bathed in an oddly coloured light. When Queen Isabella and King Ferdinand visited this sanctuary in the fifteenth century they wanted to take them away but the mule charged with their transportation refused to budge and this was taken as a divine command for them to stay put here in Cebrero.

We can again see from such stories, I think, how the Celtic mind loved nothing more than slapping the notice of a miracle on a condemned building or investing the smallest happening with a truly epic religious dimension. There was no harm in those old Celts and it is unlikely they sat down and made it up solely for pilgrim money. Rather, it was because they just couldn't help it particularly as the Celts always adored any – or all – acts of the imagination.

Tell them a nice story in a nice way – over the hearth, perhaps, with a smile on your lips and a cup of warm tea in your hand, and, ergo, it became true. It certainly didn't matter in the slightest it didn't correspond with any of our modern understanding of the workings of reality or the facts as they are. What are a few lousy facts after all?

From this we can also perhaps better understand the cult of St James since there is almost no support for it in fact. St James was a fisherman and disciple of Christ who, the Bible tells us, was beheaded by Herod. Early in the ninth century a bishop suddenly announced that his body had been discovered here in Galicia after a hermit, Pelagro, was led to the site by a great star in the sky which shone amongst a veritable field of stars. This happened on Sunday, 25 July, which became the feast day of St James the Apostle, and the cathedral was later built on this spot under this Campus Stellae, the Field of Stars – or Santiago Compostela as it became known.

The King of Spain welcomed the 'discovery' and it also emerged that the severed head and body had been brought here by ship, coming ashore at Padron. A horseman following the ship on the coastline had fallen into the sea and had drowned, only to be rescued and brought back to life by the Apostle. When the horseman came out of the sea he was festooned with scallop shells which henceforth became the emblem of this headless saint and all subsequent pilgrims.

Later the body was concealed somewhere for 800 years. Visions of St James rallied the Christians in their more or less permanent battles with the Moors. He was now the patron saint of Christian Spain and even appeared on a white charger once, complete with a sword, at a crucial stage in a battle when he decapitated numerous Moors. This, it should be pointed out, didn't quite square with the biblical characterization of James who said: 'You should

love your neighbour as yourself. Wisdom from above is first
pure, then peaceable, gentle, open to reason, full of mercy
and good fruits.'

When Sir Francis Drake threatened Galicia in 1589 the
cathedral canons were said to have hidden James' body and
then forgotten where they put it. In 1879 the remains were
found again and put on display in the cathedral. Once
again the pilgrimages prospered.

Nothing about any of these stories seems remotely true
and improbability piles on improbability. There is not even
any faint attempt to systematize the story or make it sound
slightly plausible. How, for example, might a headless corpse
get off a ship to swim to the depths of the sea to save a
horseman and then drag him out of the waves covered in
scallop shells? We've got about six different miracles running
around inside this story, each one about ten times more
miraculous than anything attempted by Christ.

No, no, no. We are here almost certainly back in the
imagination-tossed realms of wild Celtic myth where men
swim oceans with their heads under their arms and children turn into swans for centuries. These myths, then, for
whatever reason, took hold of the minds of men and, in
so doing, become absolute truth. They attained their own
force and potency and even seem to have become more
durable for actually not being true.

The small restaurant in Cebrero jangled with rattling cut-
lery and dishes being washed. In fact it was always clattery
and well patronized, I was to discover, since it was virtually
the only place in this mountain sanctuary which was reasonably warm. Many even ate their meals in here still sitting
inside their sleeping bags.

I was getting to know quite a lot of pilgrims on The
Road and, whenever we met, we would tell each other the

latest stories or exchange complaints. Dan the New Yorker kept complaining that not only was it freezing up here but also his feet were in danger of dropping off the ends of his legs. He wasn't too stuck on the food here either. Nor the Spanish.

Here I also met Wolfgang, a middle-aged German with the usual classic blond hair and shivery blue eyes. Clearly taking his task seriously he also had a scallop shell dangling around his neck on a leather thong. He was reading a paperback but seemed quite happy to answer my questions in good English when I explained what I was up to, putting his book to one side on the table carefully and giving me all his steady, blue-eyed attention.

A pilgrimage like this was a chance to rebuild yourself, he said with a certain grim earnestness which I immediately found a bit worrying. Not to rebuild your body, you must understand, but your mind and attitudes. You get to find out all the negative things about yourself on a pilgrimage and you must throw them away. He had even sat down and listed all his faults on a sheet of paper the other day and buried the list beneath a rock under a pilgrim cross so that he could leave them behind.

Ah so, this is the way it works in Alcoholics Anonymous, I told him. Every night you talk about all your bad traits in a group so that, with the help of the group, you can recognize them, deal with them and leave them behind. A man can only face life without a drink when he has developed his inner spiritual core, they say in AA. You can only develop this inner spiritual core when you have got rid of your many faults and fully understood the nature of the disease which is imprisoning you.

He looked hard at me as I spoke and I recognized that look from hundreds of other interviews I have conducted over the years, particularly when I have opened my own big mouth. This was the frosty, pained look which said: 'Hey,

I'm supposed to be the one who's doing all the talking here. Why don't you just shut up and put all my fine words down in your notebook? You might even get to learn something interesting and important.'

Well, I did shut up and learned something really interesting even if it wasn't exactly important. Wolfgang had done this pilgrimage five times before, he said, four of them with his wife. But no amount of questioning would get him to reveal what had happened to this wife. He simply kept changing the subject when I tried to solve the mystery of his matrimonial status, talking about how he had once taken a holiday in Albania which he hoped would never happen again and even, at one stage, boasting about the size and value of his stamp collection. His wife could even have run off with the milkman but, as he wasn't saying, it wasn't for me to know.

Yet I did get the feeling he was hurting quite badly, as the Californians might say. There was a pain deep within him which was almost certainly to do with his missing wife, but that was as far as I was going to get since he was now on the subject of President Clinton and not about to move off it for a long while yet.

Later that morning, in the restaurant, Dan introduced me to two vivacious young Dutch girls, Wendy and Marjorie from Amsterdam, who were both so fit you could tell they practically ate up the miles each day with lots of energy left over for the nights. Unburdened by the remotest sense of the conventional – as are most of the young Dutch I have met, even if the elderly staunchly Protestant Dutch practically invented convention – Wendy cheerfully and disarmingly said that what she liked most about doing the pilgrimage was that you could make love a lot if you found the right kind of man. 'These *refugios* get so cold and you need to keep warm somehow. Sex keeps you going too. If your man has got well ahead of you there is nothing better for keeping you going to catch up with him again. We are all like salmon, I think.'

She wasn't – as befitted a pilgrim who thought she was a salmon – remotely religious and even resented it highly, she said, when, back in León, the nuns in one *refugio* had caught her still in bed after everyone else had left one morning and all but frog-marched her to Mass. 'If they catch you in bed one minute after nine o'clock you have to go to Mass. No excuses. You can say you are sick but you have to be pretty damned sick to avoid the Mass. It is just impossible to argue with a nun since they take you by the elbow and lead you into the service.'

'So what would happen if the nuns caught you in bed with a man? Lots of Masses then, I guess.'

Both of them whinnied with laughter. 'Well, to be honest, neither of us have met a man this trip. We have not liked the look of anyone. We are very fussy, you know. *Very fussy.*'

I had lunch with Dan and was about to get on my way when I noticed that Wolfgang was sitting with Wendy and Marjorie. A lot of merriment was erupting from the table and, when Wolfgang caught my curious look, he gave me a broad and lascivious smile which, in itself, I thought, told me a lot about what had gone wrong with his marriage. You can always tell a lot about a man by the way he reacts to the company of pretty young girls and another part of Wolfgang's problem was he was simply too good-looking. No girl could possibly keep her head after looking into those big, blue eyes and I guessed that one of those Dutch girls was going to get warm again very soon.

About half an hour later I was sitting in the back of my camper writing up some notes when Wolfgang came knocking. 'You must not go,' he said. 'You must stay. I need you to stay here with me and we will make some spaghetti for the Dutch girls. I am brilliant at spaghetti.'

'I don't understand.'

'I need another man. I cannot handle both of them. Stay and we will have some fun. Wendy likes you. She says she has never had a writer. I will have Marjorie.'

'It's just not possible, Wolfgang,' I said snapping my notebook shut, a traditional reporter's indication that the interview is over. 'I've really got to finish this trip before I run out of money.'

'A day will not make any difference. What difference will a day make? I will be very upset if you leave now.'

'I'm sorry. But not half as upset as my wife will be if I stay.'

I, then, as they used to say in the *News of the World*, made my excuses and left. But I had, at least, worked out the nature of Wolfgang's problem. It is simply impossible to maintain a happy marriage and chase other girls around. That is almost the very first rule of them all.

Those pilgrim crosses came thick and fast after I left Cebrero and, in Triacestella, I came across a high cairn of stones with a small statue on top of it. Pilgrims had once been asked to carry a stone from here to the kilns of Castaneda where it would be converted into lime to help in the rebuilding of the cathedral in Compostela.

Every garden out this way had a *horreo*, a strange, oblong structure made of slatted stone or wood and mounted on stilts. At first I thought it was some kind of private family vault since they were always festooned with crosses but it turned out they were small granaries, built to protect the grain from rats or birds and to keep it well-aired or dry.

The real family vaults in the cemeteries were also interesting since they were built in long rows of concrete drawers piled on top of one another in tiers of three or four rather like a left luggage office. Each drawer had a big, iron handle on it and, although probably only big enough for one, I guessed most of the family must have gone in there sooner or later. I've long had a thing about cemeteries and arrangements for the dead so I tried to get a closer look at these drawers a few times but always found the grounds locked.

This countryside might almost have been from another world again, what with the wild horses foraging on the high slopes and women trundling along the pavements balancing stooks of hay on their heads. The fields had also been chopped into small parcels of land with their borders marked out by rough, triangular stones which had been crudely wired together. Light brown cows broke off their chewing to look up. The dull chimes of their bells haunted every dark night and always there were large birds of prey circling those great drizzling skies looking for something to prey on. Eagles were the emblems of Jupiter, the god of the skies.

Small orange gas canisters sat outside the homes waiting to be picked up and many of the lanes were choked up with groaning tractors. I passed a house with a room for the cow next to the kitchen, just as they had once had in nineteenth-century Wales. Later I saw a woman leading a bull by hand by a ring in his nose.

I also passed another house with a man standing in the doorway looking out and his eyes were but small pools of red, with no other colour in them at all, just two matching pools of burst red veins. That fiery look followed me for quite a few miles before it went away again although, even weeks later, it still kept coming back at odd moments. The man with the red eyes.

Rain came again and it didn't fall haphazardly or as some vaporous afterthought by some passing cloud but uniformly and determinedly, all the time, without pause or taking a breath, soaking everything in sight and, in case we hadn't got the message the first time, roundly soaking us all again. This was real Celtic rain, seeping into every inch of you, seeping into your clothes and right into every bone, seeping into your deepest flesh and thought, seeping into the very floor of your soul in the damp, rainy way that I had always thought only happened in the middle of darkest, wettest Wales.

The camp site in Portomarin was high on a hill and overlooking a lake where they had recently drowned a village to make way for a reservoir. The ruins of the village could still be seen, I was told, when the water level was low, next to the arch which still survives of the old Romanesque bridge, the Puente Mina. That chapel over there was called Santa Maria of the Snows which had also just escaped being flooded along with the valley. We Welsh, who have honours degrees in rain, also know about flooded villages and valleys, often to provide water for the English. Drowned villages have become a part of our folklore and again I was surprised at how closely and intimately my own Welsh spirit was finding itself at home here in Galicia.

The field in which I was camping was more like a moving bog with the rain coming down so heavily that, after putting up their tent, my two Dutch friends, Sophie and Thyss, had moved over to the corrugated shelter where Sophie was busy cooking the evening meal on their primus with her usual fag in her mouth and Thyss was busy trying to open yet another carton of wine.

Later I wandered over to the bar on the camp site where we sat and watched a Wimbledon tennis match on the television, all being played out in the most glorious sunshine. You didn't need a tennis match or a pop concert or eleven men in whites to make it rain in Galicia since here it clearly rained all the time.

10

The Swinging Botafumeiro

It was early on a Sunday morning and I was sitting in a bright patch of sunlight on the cobbles of the Plaza de España in Santiago de Compostela with the huge cathedral behind me and surrounded by an expensive *parador*, the Archbishop's Palace and the Artists' College.

Faint sounds of jubilation kept spinning through the sunlight such as distant fiesta horns since this square marked the end of The Road; here the pilgrim declared there was nothing more to be accomplished and there were no more meandering tracks to stumble along. Here that long and painful story of the *Camino* concluded with a little lightening of the heart and a wobble of triumph.

Bagpipe music was wheezing away in some distant alley and sellers of Galician souvenirs and lottery tickets were moving around me. A musician was selling tapes of Celtic music and a dog was togged up in Galician national costume. A party of about 30 young schoolgirls, all in navy blue skirts and white shirts, came singing out of a nearby square and once they reached the cathedral steps they began dancing in a collective spasm of spontaneous happiness which, as far as I could see, had nothing to do with the teacher who was leading them. They were just glad to be here.

Everything about this morning in Santiago was perfect

and it was as if I had ordered my own personal hour of
Spanish sunlight, together with my own chair and favourite
music, before sitting down right in the middle of a painting
by Brueghel, admiring in particular the interplay of sunshine
with shadow, the subtle way the artist had introduced gra-
dations of light as it reached over those cobbles. I wouldn't
have changed the positions of any of the principal figures
in this painting either; they were about right where they
were.

A few more pilgrims, thumbs locked in the straps of
their back-packs, came striding over the square, walking the
last few yards of a journey of a few thousand miles. You
could see the joy and relief in the spring of their steps; in
the way they shook hands with one another or, on occasion,
hugged one another. Several women looked up at the high,
thrilling face of the cathedral and burst into tears. These
were the tears of people who had finally done something
tough and even courageous; people who had reached deep
into their reserves and found something which they
thought they had long lost.

Another two rucksacked men were practically running
across the square towards the cathedral without looking up
or around them. They were dirty and bristled, brown all
over and caked with mud in parts. These were the hard
men of The Road, the ones who tackled each and every
day relentlessly and without flinching, no matter what the
weather, without recourse to taxis or bikes or little engines
attached to the back wheels. You knew, without even
touching them, those muddy leg muscles had the feel of
iron and their calves were as tough and big as old sides of
beef. .

Three more arrived who took off their back-packs and lay
back on the cobbles, hands under their smiling heads as
they looked up at the dazzling face of this lustrous cathedral.
This was like no other cathedral I had ever seen, a barmy

collection of ornamental arches and spires, each one improbably balanced on the top of the other and soaring up into Spanish skies with all the flamboyant panache of a flamenco dancer.

The blackened stonework was delicately patterned with orange splashes of lichen and a variety of weeds grew profusely in the many cracks and crevices. A lot of the exuberant towers also seemed out of true and, such was the profusion of balcony, pyramid, head and flower everywhere, the whole facade seemed to vibrate like a field of stone flowers in a light wind. The architectural word for all this is churrigueresque, a word with a wonderful Dixieland strut to it which means an extremely ornate fashion of baroque architecture. Churrigueresque. Someone should at the very least write a book with that in the title. *Heartbreak Thy Name is Churrigueresque. Forever Churrigueresque. How Churrigueresque Was My Valley.*

More pilgrims were crowding in through the Romanesque doorway – the *Portico de la Gloria* – whose roof and walls were amok with many forms of carving depicting everything from the details of the Crucifixion to the Last Judgement. St James himself, looking more than a little fed up, stood at the top of one pillar where there was an impression of four fingers and a thumb left in the stone by the hands of millions of pilgrims over the years.

I put my hand in there too, connecting briefly in a smooth touch of warm stone, with all those who had gone before me on the long road of St James. Once inside I found the pews were already full with hundreds crowding the aisles and milling around many abandoned back-packs since, in about twenty minutes, the Sunday morning Mass for pilgrims was about to begin.

There is nothing special – or churrigueresque – about your first sight of Compostela and some have even recorded recoiling with horror at the sight of the city and wanting to go straight back home again. The first of any pilgrim group to crest the hill and see the cathedral spires was supposed to shout 'Mountjoie' whereupon he would be declared king of the group and thereafter be known as Le Roy. But, in truth, our modern Le Roy would only have seen a most miserable sight with the cathedral spires just about poking above a sprawl of high-rise blocks and light industrial estates. Garages sat cheek by jowl with supermarkets. Car rental offices sat among the aerials of a large television studio.

Yet, as you penetrated the city, you found yourself moving around the back of huge old monastic settlements, shuffling along old cobbled lanes and looking up at high windows, wondering what went on behind them. These old streets have the smell of Jerusalem about them and, long before you actually get to the cathedral, you do get an increasingly powerful feeling that you are connecting with one of the world's spiritual power points.

The cobbled lanes had lots of fish restaurants in them as they twisted down towards the square. I sometimes stopped and stared through their windows at the luckless lobsters on display on silver platters, their claws tied with elastic bands and mouths opening and closing as their feelers waved around semaphoring clear signals of extreme distress.

I saw a couple pick their own lobster but, as I have long known, here in Spain you are not bound to get the one you pick. In Almeria I once saw a lobster being fished out of a tank and when I later found myself around the rear of the restaurant I poked my head into the kitchen, wondering if lobsters really did scream when they were boiled, but was never to find out because the waiter was standing in front of the open doors of the deep freeze where he was holding up the live lobster and looking for a suitable match in the pile of deep-frozen ones in front of him.

I also found a lot of churches in the old town, jammed

with unbelievable treasures and a really sharp pilgrim museum, detailing the history of the city and the cathedral as well as the life and times of St James. Just around one corner was a delightful, dusty shop where four men were painting religious statuary – all of them sitting quietly as if they were about to take communion as they painted the red lips of Our Lady or the white robes of a saint or the purple flowers of a handmaiden.

Lots of fire crackers were going off the day I arrived with a constant beeping of car horns, announcing some fevered fiesta in some distant suburb below that low line of eucalyptus-dotted mountains.

The part of the old town scattered around the cathedral had been pedestrianized and it was a brave man who tried to drive his car in here. Almost every corner had its own resident policeman who, complete with sunglasses and guns, flagged down approaching vehicles before ordering them to leave again even when they tried to claim they had official permission and produced documents to prove it. Out.

Yet as I sloped around these streets I came across an unreal air of friendliness because, even though I had not set foot in this city before, I forever found myself shaking hands with the boys or kissing the girls whom I had met over the previous few months on The Road.

I also spent a lot of time with Sophie and Thyss who kept remarking on how empty and flat they felt after completing their long journey, which confirmed what I have long believed: the journey is everything and the arrival often a let-down. They also told me they had heard an interesting story of sin and redemption concerning a couple of delinquents who had been ordered by the courts to make this pilgrimage to Compostela. They had been hauled up before the magistrate in Holland on an assault charge and ordered to make the pilgrimage on foot with a policeman instead of being thrown in the jug. Only when they returned with their pilgrim passports fully stamped would the magistrate consider letting them off. I'm sure it would have been far easier for them if they'd opted for the jug but I never managed to catch up with them to find out. Maybe they had thought better of it and done a runner.

Then, one afternoon, I met Wolfgang as we were both browsing in the same silversmith's shop and he was not best pleased with me, grumpily announcing it had been 'No dice' with the Dutch girls and how it would probably have been a lot different for him if I had stayed back with him in Cebrero. Anyway, he was going home the following morning when he would be re-united with his wife who, he revealed at last, was on a pilgrimage of her own. To Fatimah.

I also met Dan the New Yorker who was fretting he had told me something which he absolutely didn't want to show up in any book I might write about the pilgrimage. The trouble was, despite much discussion, neither of us could quite remember what it might be he did not want to appear in cold print, so it could not have been all that important.

All these pilgrims at some time or other ended up in the office where they were issued with *compostelles* on production of their fully stamped passports. This *compostelle* could also be exchanged for a free meal in the *parador* next to the cathedral although the woman in the passport office told me the *parador* now only gave out free meals to six pilgrims a day *and* they had to eat them in the servants' quarters. This same woman did make my day complete, however, when, after learning what I was up to, she told me not only had she bought *Landscapes of Glory*, my previous book, *but had actually read it*. This really was something of a first since not only do my friends or acquaintances rarely buy any book of mine but, even when I give them one free, they still usually can't be bothered to read the thing. One once admitted he had not even got around to reading the words on the dust cover.

A strange mood of aggravation was skittering around the pews before the start of the Pilgrim Mass in the cathedral in Santiago that morning which I could not quite understand. It was something, I think, to do with a sense of frustration between the visiting pilgrims, who were tetchy and tired after walking for so long to get there and the local Galicians who, rightly or wrongly, regarded the cathedral as their own.

Certainly one elderly Galician woman told me to beat it with a few sharp jerks of her thumb when I tried to sit in an empty space next to her and, a few rows back, there was the mother and father of all arguments going on between four Galicians who had taken the pew which had been booked by some young Spanish pilgrims who, having left their back-packs on it, had gone off to look around the cathedral. They had come back to find their back-packs dumped in the aisle with the others and the four Galicians arguing something along the lines that, as they had left their seats, it was too bad. You can't book a pew with a back-pack, they seemed to be saying.

A lot of swearing and unseemly cussing was going on, sucking in members of the congregation all around who were also berating the Galicians for taking the seats of the *peregrinos*, particularly now the other pews were full. At this sticky moment a procession of white-robe priests came down the aisle following a Processional Cross and they had to pick their way through the abandoned back-packs as the swearing and cussing reached new heights, even if the one Galician man, who had earlier seemed at the epicentre of this particular storm, now had his eyes closed and his hands locked together prayerfully as the Mass was about to begin. I could not understand how someone could pray so fervently moments after stealing someone else's pew.

I managed to squeeze in next to a man who was not at all happy about having to move his own back-pack and giant stave with his water bottle and scallop shells dangling off it, muttering to himself in deep irritation. I don't think I've ever known such bad vibes going on in a holy place and just prior to a religious service. Everyone seemed to have the hump about something or other and, to make matters worse, the body odour was horrendous in what must have been the smelliest, most ragged, most irritable – if not the fittest – congregation which has ever come together to praise the Lord.

But the praise wasn't starting now, not just yet since the arguments were still going on with those four Galicians. The main man, who was still praying, got a sharp poke in his back and, for one appalling moment, he broke off his prayer with his hands bunching into fists and I really did think a huge fight was going to break out there and then.

Now, in a further bizarre twist, one of the tourists with a video camera had followed the procession right up to the High Altar, where he was filming each of the priests as they took up their positions, until one of them shooed him away again. This Mass was going to end up something like a football riot unless everyone settled down.

Everyone did finally settle down when the officiating priest began singing a song of welcome to the pilgrims with sections of the congregation joining in uncertainly. A further speech of welcome was followed by another hymn and a long and meandering sermon, in Spanish, about the meaning of the pilgrimage to Compostela. I think.

As the sermon continued meandering like the slowest river on the hottest day of the year my eyes wandered around the cathedral's high and barrel-vaulted nave. Every corner teemed with beauty and elegance as befitted a building created by the Catholic Church at the height of her power and influence. Each of the chapels around the sides was a shadowy place of statuary and prayer and my eyes finally came to rest on the huge and opulent High Altar which was such a jumble of so many things – of gold and silver, of darkness and light – it took some time to work out what was what. But, with this priest delivering the sermon, time was something I had a lot of.

A huge gilt canopy was held up by even larger angels on the High Altar. A mass of chandeliers, crosses, flowers and guttering candles crowded together as haphazardly as in a busy antique shop and, right in the middle of this Aladdin's Cave, was a statue of St James looking quite pleased with himself, as well he might surrounded by all these riches.

Yet, unless my eyes were playing tricks on me, I kept spotting fluttery movements around the whereabouts of St James' shoulders. Occasionally a head – as in human head – seemed to rest on one of his shoulders only to disappear again into that golden jumble of treasures. Arms reached out to clutch his neck. It was almost as if a bunch of people had got themselves imprisoned in a cage behind the High Altar, perhaps for fighting in the pews, and were now trying to escape. What with the near-fight minutes earlier this was turning out to be some strange cathedral. So what was up behind the High Altar?

I was only later to discover that, as well as putting your hand in that pillar in the porchway, pilgrims were also encouraged to ascend some stairs behind the High Altar where they could kiss and cuddle the back of the statue of St James – even in the middle of Mass.

The sermon did finally come to an end and it was followed by communion when we trooped up in a more or less orderly fashion to take our wafer. In fact we were all queueing quietly when, surprise, surprise, that elderly Spanish woman, who had given me the heave-ho from the seat next to her, came barging past us to get to the priest and her wafer first, moving through us like a policeman taking charge of a nasty incident before holding up her hands slowly and with exaggerated reverence as if the whole of the service and indeed the cathedral had been built solely for her.

That tourist with his appalling video camera joined the line of communicants and there was a brief stand-off as the priest held out the wafer to him and he just stood there videoing the priest's proffered hand. The priest waggled the wafer around and lifted his eyebrows into one question: Are you going to take this from me or are you going to stand there filming me all morning?

That tourist with his video camera probably wouldn't have got away with this in Jerusalem, particularly in the Church of the Holy Sepulchre, where I have actually seen the priests shove and hit pilgrims when they have begun getting out of control. But this probably wouldn't have been a terribly clever idea here since, judging from what I had seen of the mood of this congregation, if a priest hit someone in this cathedral, he would probably get hit straight back again and the ensuing fight would carry on until next Christmas.

Moments of untidy confusion followed communion as we tried to find our seats again, climbing over back-packs and staves, when the whole building shook to the heart-stopping burst of an organ. Everyone surged forward as the *Botafumeiro* – or giant silver censer – was carried in on a pole on the shoulders of two men. This censer was about the size of a Sumo wrestler and it was opened and the incense inside it lit.

Some eight men in red robes began hauling this giant silver mass up into the air on an intricate series of ropes and the higher they pulled it the greater its swing. It was the most spectacular and theatrical sight I have ever seen in a cathedral as the censer swung ever higher back and forth across the transept, now at the peak of its swing as it practically touched the ceiling on either side.

The priests on the High Altar had moved closer to the arc of the swing, some ascending the pulpits for a better view. The rush of air fanned the burning incense into furious flames as the *Botafumeiro* swung through a 180 degree arc. Despite its size, it made little sound as it kept swinging up into the high shafts of sunshine even though it trailed long wisps of smoke behind it like a crash-landing Spitfire. Children cried out and covered their eyes. Mouths dropped open. The priests, who had obviously seen it a thousand times before, smiled.

Traditionally the *Botafumeiro* was used to symbolically fumigate the pilgrims after their long and smelly walk. Somewhat amazingly no one had ever been seriously injured by it, despite the definitely medieval air of those ropes, although it did once hit the roof awkwardly and fell apart many years ago.

The men on the ropes broke its swing and it started getting slower and slower after its furious, flaming and positively awe-inspiring flight. Someone finally stepped in its way and a loud burst of applause followed as it was unclipped from the ropes and shouldered out again by the same two men. The Mass broke up into such an unruly milling crowd that not even the priests on the High Altar could get out properly, stuck in the middle of everything like cricketers caught in a cheering crowd at the end of a triumphant match.

But you could see the priests were used to it. They didn't pull faces or mutter about indignities. They knew all about this odd pilgrim Mass and the way it attracted the strangest mixture of the proprietorial local, the worn-out

and the smelly, the fractious and the rude. Priests know
all there is to know about the failings of ordinary people
especially when they are at the end of their tether.

It would have been right and proper, I guess, to have ended
my pilgrimage with the swinging of the *Botafumeiro* except
that it did not end there. Rather, it ended a few days later
when I was staying in Finisterre, on the Galician coast.

Finisterre is a small huddle of grey buildings wedged into
a lot of rocks and surrounded by a sea which keeps bursting
against the rocks in the usual primordial and rhythmic way.
Even as a town it has almost no consequence and I was
resting up here for a while on a camp site before making
my way home again.

I had been out walking and stood on the nearby head-
land for a while, watching the sun sink for a final time, here
in a place which the early Celts once regarded as the End
of the World. I wondered about the millions of pilgrims
who must have watched the same sight before me accompanied only by the sounds of the visiting waves.

The evening was warm and dry, by way of a novel
change, and I found myself looking up at a huge canopy of
darkness, nailed to heaven itself by thousands of glittering
stars. A shooting star – an angel going about its business,
I've often thought – fell the length of the night, and there
was another and another. From somewhere nearby came
the sound of a guitar and lots of laughter.

Nothing is quite so humbling as looking up at a great
night sky awash with stars and galaxies which, between
them, pose billions of questions to which we have barely one
single answer. A field of stars is almost a complete statement
of the majesty and complexity of God. We can get some
idea of his very bigness by looking at the stars, and I've
always understood why the ancients regarded the sky as the

great world book and why they saw the stars as the letters and the constellations the words and sentences of this book. As the stars moved so the story changed and unfolded. Those ancients completely understood the concepts of mystery, wonder and worship. They knew stars were the tallow candles of the Celtic soul which would lead us through our long, dark nights, finally taking us all home to God just as they did for the Magi. It was also a star which led that hermit to the sarcophagus containing the remains of St James.

And as I stood there, with my face buffeted by the warm sea breezes and my eyes filled with this glittering wonder, I began thinking of the pilgrims I had met over the previous few months and I saw them, in my mind's eye, continuing their long pilgrimage along a new stretch of The Road which was, in its turn, now taking them up to the very stars.

They were all there – the blonde German boys with their blue eyes and long legs; the dumpy French girls, shoulders hunched with a steely determination; the Spanish family leading their blind father; the member of the House of Lords; Wolfgang who had lost his wife and Frans, the Dutch policeman who had found his new love; Dan the New Yorker and the Mayor and the Architect. There were also the more peripheral characters – the lorry driver knocked down by his own runaway wheel; Helmut the Snorer; the Dutch juvenile delinquents; and those four priests making their way along The Road and cleansing it with their prayers.

And as I saw them picking their way through this field of stars, with their pilgrim staves and floppy hats, I also saw them walking right through the gates of thanksgiving and into the courts of praise of God Himself. These pilgrims – whether they knew it or not and whether they wanted to or not – had taken the long hard road into pain which, in its turn, had taken them close to the mind and heart of God.

They had given up the best hours of their lives to The Road which will always be strong and always be holding them on its back as they walk along its length. So The Road, then, also becomes a metaphor for God Himself as He carries us, tests us, looks for our weaknesses, finds us out, understands us and discovers what we are capable of as we struggle on, through fair weather and foul, with no tangible or obvious rewards on offer. We can cheat, we can go by taxi or by bus but we can never cheat him because he knows every single thing about us. No one understands our frailty better than him; no one knows better how we are forever seeking out the line of least resistance.

But, as he gets to know us on The Road, then so too we get to know him because, as we travel on, we also create him in our minds. We are forever taking the raw materials of The Road and using them to add to our knowledge of him. We see those lines of pilgrims making their ways through vineyards which smell of ice cream; we see again those multicoloured wild flowers lining The Road through Castile; we hear again the hollow drumming sounds of the storks of Logroño, the nickering of wild horses and the sound of cow bells in those damp, Galician nights; we smell again the smoke as the farmers clear their fields of stubble with fire. All these images and smells tell us about God.

Out on The Road we also clothed him in the daily miracles of an ordinary world; we bathed him in the cold mountain streams and saw his very face in the fish in the clean loveliness of all those pilgrim rivers. We built him out of the sunlight in a room in a ruined monastery and the memories of all those we have loved and lost. We actually put him together in the quickening pulse of the morning and dying fall of the night; out of the clouds and the swelling birdsong that greets every dawn.

We also caught sight of him in the soaring arches of all those cathedrals, which were built out of such a deep and rich faith; we met him in the monks and all those foot doctors of the *Camino*; in the eyes of children and the red eyes of that Galician peasant staring out onto his own world. It got that he was almost everywhere we turned and we knew we were being enfolded by him and cared for by him just as, when we really needed him, he spoke to us, not in torrents of fire or bolts of lightning, but as you would expect the Father of Christ to speak, quietly and directly, through the image of that Belsen wraith at Lourdes; that ruined child who said I should fear nothing and that it could be a thousand times worse since I could be just like him. *Just like him!*

So we have here the moments, the sights, the smells and the very language of pilgrimage which are forever adding to – or replenishing – our love relationship with God. Out on The Road we are entering his very heart and he becomes our controlling force. When we worship him we are also worshipping all that is beautiful in the world; we are worshipping the inherent beauty of life itself.

As I stood there at the End of the World, hearing the sounds of the waves and seeing lines of pilgrims making their way through a field of stars, I came to understand the meaning of this great pilgrimage to Santiago de Compostela which might indeed have little basis in historical fact but is a way of bringing us closer to God just as he then becomes closer to us.

At certain junctures – be it in Lourdes or Logroño or in a forest clearing in Rioja – we attain a mystical union with him which is as unexpected as it is indefinable. In those moments of glory we have found him, not through dusty theological or travel books, but out on The Road, beholding him from without and creating him from within. He was certainly here with me that night in Finisterre, standing close as we both listened to the sounds of that guitar and the laughter.

So out on The Road we can become faithful and free again; we can pick our way through a field of stars and enter his courts of praise, finding ourselves especially close to him and the meaning of life, taking nothing but what is lovely and good in his world and firing it together in a personal image of him, using only the ragged poetry of our wayward pilgrim hearts.

Also by TOM DAVIES

Wild Skies and Celtic Paths
ISBN 0-281-05190-9

This award-winning travel book takes us on an
entertaining journey in the footsteps of medieval
pilgrims to revisit the holy places of Britain and Ireland.
With his telling eye for the offbeat and the comic, he
describes the characters he meets, the delightful and
dreadful places he visits, the diversity of the landscape
and the changing seasons. In a style that will surprise
and delight the faithful and the lapsed alike, he shows
how the spirit of pilgrimage and the faithfulness that
inspires it are far from dead.

Landscapes of Glory
ISBN 0-281-04908-4

A magical, mystical pilgrimage around the holy
places of England by award-winning writer Tom Davies,
who sets out to track down the English soul. Are we a
people of faith? Do we still pray? This poetic and
funny account of an English odyssey will amuse and
enthrall.

The Celtic Heart
ISBN 0-281-05028-7

A visionary journey through the land and life of
the Celts. Standing alongside St Patrick at Tara, on
Iona with St Columba and joining in a Welsh revival
meeting, Davies defines the character of Celtic
spirituality, not only for the past, but in our
present and future.

'His wonderfully documented journey through the
lands of *The Celtic Heart* is hilarious and moving;
blunt and poignant; heart-warming and chilling – all
at the same time.'
Christianity

TRIANGLE

Available from all good bookshops